# Lead in Light of Eternity

# Lead in Light of Eternity

## The Jesus Model

STACY RINEHART

# What Leaders Are Saying

A truly excellent book! In an age obsessed with fast followers, fame, and fortune, Stacy openly and transparently invites us to face the reality of Jesus—His life, His ministry, His strategy, His method. From decades of hard-won experience, Stacy hits the nail squarely on the head. Read this book, and encourage every Christian leader you know to read this book!

**Malcolm Webber, PhD**
Founder and Executive Director, LeaderSource SGA

Here is one of the best books on leadership I have ever read. From a wealth of extensive study and years of practical experience, Stacy Rinehart explodes standard clichés and directs the reader to Jesus's way of effective leadership. Be warned! *Lead in Light of Eternity* will turn you inside out and upside down. Read this book and your life will never be the same.

**Ron Blue, PhD**
Coordinator, Spanish DMin Program
Dallas Theological Seminary

Beware leaders…Read with caution…Life-changing principles and concepts lie ahead…This is a timely book that needs to be read, pondered, and applied by the Body of Christ. And here is why…All cultures are marred by sin, including our own culture and its concepts and models of leadership. The kingdom culture supersedes them all and is designed to permeate and infiltrate all cultures of the world. Stacy's book leads us through this maze with a radical new way of thinking, living, and leading in the kingdom culture as it confronts the cultures of the world. This style of kingdom leadership does not compete with culture—it confronts it. Stacy is very transparent in his attempt to live and practice this style of leadership. He brings together a powerful book in describing how to practically put these concepts and principles into practice.

**Dr. Terry Taylor**
President Emeritus, US Navigators

*Lead in Light of Eternity* is a new way of thinking that takes leadership to the foundational levels of character and kingdom focus. My friend, Stacy Rinehart, opens his heart and his life experiences, filtered through scripture, to paint a picture of a new kind of leader—one who leads out of spiritual depth and Spirit-anointed giftedness. This is not a "quick read" or a "quick fix." These concepts will take root in your life and leadership only if they become part of your spiritual DNA. This happens by thoughtful study and prayer and a deep willingness to grow and change. This book is a must-read for every leader.

**Jerry E. White, PhD**
Major General, USAF, retired
International President Emeritus, The Navigators

*Lead in Light of Eternity,* is an absolute essential for anyone in any level of leadership—home, small group, church, or ministry. It's a fresh, up-close look at the core of Jesus, the ultimate leader.

**Phill Butler**
Senior Strategy Advisor, VisionSynergy

In a time characterized by self-promoting, self-propagating, power-dominating, money-seeking, and man-centered leadership, Dr. Stacy unveils for us the secret of authentic and fruitful Christian life, ministry, and leadership. This book will change your leadership. Not only will it change your leadership, it will change you. I highly recommend it.

**Reverend-Pastor Pierre Celestin NTOKO**
Bible Teacher, Mission Mobilizer, Cameroon

This book should be required reading for anyone who aspires to lead in the secular world.

**Hendrik Struik**
International Director, Eli Lilly and Company (Retired)

When authors can challenge their readers to rethink the ways they've operated in the past, they are truly excellent. Stacy has done just that; he has challenged my leadership style and encouraged me to rethink how I lead.

**Allin Foulkrod, CSEP**
President, Creative Visions

*Lead in Light of Eternity* steps out to address two significant issues often bypassed by writers, preachers, and teachers, that of "False Teachers" and "Organizationalism—The Pervasive Idol." These two chapters alone make for instructive reading to enhance our personal mentoring ministry.

**Myron S. Harrison**
OMF (Retired)

*Lead in Light of Eternity* has the feel of a fireside conversation with a spiritual father whose love and prophetic voice convincingly charges us to walk with Jesus and lead like Him. Enjoy, ponder, and grow!

**Dr. Phil Arendt**
Associate Executive Director, Reach Global

When you have finished this book, you'll be a changed person, more in tune with the Spirit, whose heart beats for the world.

**Skip Gray**
The Navigators

A book you will reread, practice, and pass on!

**Frode Randgaard**

Mentor and Project Leader, Arrow Leadership Norway

Some books should be read for information, some for inspiration, but *Lead in Light of Eternity* should be read for life transformation. This book will change the perspective, and hopefully the reality, of every reader's life and leadership.

**Marvin Brubacher**

Executive Director, MentorLink Canada

This is by far the most godly approach to leadership I have encountered. I cannot count the number of times I read something and said to myself, "That is so simple and yet so on target. Why didn't I see that before?" Stacy's study, knowledge, and experience working across cultural borders were used by the Holy Spirit to provide an absolute must-read for anyone desiring to build God's kingdom for His glory.

**Dr. Dave Coryell**

Executive Director, Christian Endeavor Mid-Atlantic

May this small volume serve as a catalyst for the transformation of our leadership models and practices, seeking Christ above all: His character, His values, and His motives.

**Steve M. Irvin, PhD**

C&MA, Spain

This book presents leadership from a biblical perspective where character precedes competence and eternal rewards trump earthly results.

**Dr. Steve Lake**

President, Designed to Serve

In *Lead in Light of Eternity,* Stacy Rinehart focuses on the leader's relationship with God and personal character rather than skills and building personal agendas.

**Jennifer Ennis**
Cofounder, JourneyMates

If you want to honor Jesus with your heart motives, your values, your character, and by your actions, this book will provide you with an invaluable "gut check." If you simply want to follow Jesus alone in how you lead, be prepared for the challenge herein!

**Dr. Paul R. Ford**
Author, Teambuilding, and Leadership Specialist

Chapter after chapter, I was convicted, encouraged, and challenged as I read this book. Thank you, Stacy, for blessing the Body of Christ with a stimulating and Gospel-rooted picture of how to follow Jesus's way of leadership.

**Brian Float**
President, Kingdom Rain

In a generation trapped by the culture of theater and glamour, Stacy's book, *Lead in Light of Eternity,* comes as a wake-up call to all twenty-first-century Christian leaders, especially emerging leaders. A timely guide to all who have eternity in view, and a must-read for emerging African leaders in both church and public life.

**Dibankap Benvictor OjongManyiNkongho**
Board Chair, DAI-Cameroon

I welcome Stacy's initiative to write this book and look forward with great anticipation to the impact it will have in the lives of those who read it. I am convinced that by reading this book, the readers will fully benefit from the experience and knowledge passed on through it.

**Petru Bulica**
Senior Pastor, First Baptist Church Betel, Timisoara, Romania

*Lead in Light of Eternity* is an essential book for leaders of all types, from those who lead churches and ministries to men and women who lead in their jobs, homes, and local communities.

**Dr. Camille Bishop**
Assistant Provost, University of the Nations

This book is a timely addition for many across the world who battle to move from the left to the right. This book will greatly help in shaping cultures essential for missional purpose.

**Dr. Joshua Pillai**
Executive, Global Church Planting Network, Bangalore, India

Stacy has written a book on perspective for Christian leaders. As leaders we need to grasp the ultimate leader's priorities and procedures. This book shows us both. Also, we need confirmation and new encouragement. This book gives us both. It is eye-opening, inspiring, and practical. I have already read it several times. I will surely reread it soon and pick up even more wisdom and tools from it.

**Ole K. Gulbrandsen**
Christian Businessman and Church Leader, Norway

Underneath Stacy's presentation of leadership is a clear and sound understanding of the kingdom of God, an apt foundation for building a biblical view of leadership. This book will prepare you not only to lead in a kingdom way but also for the day you stand before the King and give an account of how you led.

**Eddie Broussard Jr.**
International Vice President, The Navigators

Stacy Rinehart writes from more than forty years of fruitful experience of leading leaders in the global church to follow Jesus. His book reflects his deep commitment to understand and practice leadership that conforms to the example of Jesus. His book will serve as a helpful, practical guide for leaders of the worldwide church as they seek to follow Jesus in their ministry.

**Walter Hansen**
Rivendell Stewards' Trust

Most people in the world want to be leaders or develop leaders but do not know how. *Lead in Light of Eternity* teaches us how a leader can be successful in Jesus's kingdom and leave behind a transformed society. Dr. Stacy provides us with an excellent and comprehensive model of what it means to be a leader who understands and leads Jesus's way. This is a book to read. It will change you and your world.

**Dr. Aila Tasse**
Founder and President,
Lifeway Mission International (Nairobi, Kenya)

Honest and pointed, but not despairing, Rinehart calls us to something more than popularity, convenience, and managerial prowess; it might be called holiness.

**Allan Poole**
Senior Pastor, Blacknall Presbyterian Church

Stacy awakens in us the truth that only those living like Jesus and leading like Jesus will ultimately receive the eternal blessings of Jesus. All who lead will someday have their personal "Faithfulness Review" by the Master. This book will help us prepare for that moment with humble yet joyful anticipation.

**Dr. Bill Fietje**
President, Associated Gospel Churches
Burlington Ontario, Canada

I recommend and endorse *Lead in Light of Eternity* by Dr Stacy Rinehart as a strategic book and resource to help leaders in Sub-Saharan Africa to evaluate their leadership and compare it to kingdom values.

**Rene Mbongo**
West Africa Director, Partners International

*Lead in Light of Eternity* will transform your understanding, and just maybe your practice, of leadership. Stacy will show you that Jesus lived and taught an inside-out way of leading that can change the lives of fallen human beings. I encourage you to open yourself up to the Jesus way of leadership.

**Floyd Green**
Founder and CEO, Cornerstone Wealth Management

*Lead in Light of Eternity* is a call to discipleship and mentoring…These principles, prayerfully applied, will inspire you to lead like Jesus. Stacy offers us a wealth of wisdom and experience accumulated over years of real life testimonies from true servant leaders around the world.

**D. M. Rusty Moore Jr.**
Chairman and CEO, Cherry Financial Partners

*Lead in Light of Eternity* reflects the values, experience, knowledge, and humility that has been evident throughout Stacy's ministry life. Thank you, Stacy, for expressing these things so simply.

**Chuck Holland, MD**

*Lead in Light of Eternity* challenges us to be transformed to a focus on kingdom, grace, service, collaboration, and developing others. Building on his vast experience in training Christian leaders, Stacy shares practical tools for evaluating how well we are doing in following Jesus and for helping us grow to be and to lead more like Him. Stacy challenges our idols of success, size, and organizational consistency. This is not a comfortable book, but it is an important one.

**Erick Schenkel, PhD**
Executive Director, The *JESUS* Film Project

Stacy has given us an enjoyable and easy-to-apply leadership development manual that cuts across gender, culture, and generational divide. His treatment of the core-value shift and the realities of kingdom leaders is unassuming and yet profound. If leading inside out brings cleansing to the inner life of a leader, the power model of Jesus strengthens the doggedness of a leader with eternity in view to lead with kingdom pursuit, just as Jesus did. I want this book read worldwide by all who are grooming leaders or offering leadership service in the Body of Christ.

**Timothy O. Olonade**
Founder, Mentor Development Network, Africa
Former Executive Secretary, Nigeria Evangelical
Missions Association

The best gifts often come in small packages. In *Leading in Light of Eternity,* Stacy Rinehart has created a gem that is concise and pithy and adaptable by a leader in any role or context. Like other jewels, it can (and should) be read and reread to mine out and digest the principles of biblical servant leadership.

**William A. Mann**
Of Counsel and Former Partner
Ragsdale Liggett, PLLC

I've been fortunate to count Stacy as a friend for over twenty years. During that time, I have come to know him as a courageous, quiet, and deeply spiritual Christ follower. His new book, *Lead in Light of Eternity*, is more a reflection of its author than one might imagine. In it Stacy pulls no punches, tackling head on the thorniest issues confronting Christian leaders today. Any serious reader will turn its final page feeling challenged and convicted. And I found myself sensing the work, my work, had just begun.

**Michael Mangum**
Senior Consultant, FMI Center for Strategic Leadership

Dr. Stacy Rinehart explains in a crystal-clear way the Jesus model of leadership and how to lead from the inside out: "To lead from the inside out is to keep in fellowship with Jesus and walk in His ways, constantly checking our heart, looking at our character, checking our motives, and evaluating what we value in light of Jesus's values." It is a must-read book for every Christian leader, regardless his or her role, denomination, or country,

**Adel Azmy**
Assistant IDD MENA Region, Lausanne Movement

Stacy—despite his gentle and come-alongside style—grabs our attention in the introduction and continues through nine chapters to pin our attention on Jesus, the only model worth emulating into eternity. He writes out of the transformative changes and paradigm shifts he has experienced since first submitting to Jesus's Lordship in 1970. I read each page with a quiet yet dramatic sense that I was hearing words freighted with spiritual authority. Stacy points us to the Jesus model, a way that is focused on the long range and big picture; an approach that is radically committed to organic relationships rather than organizational ladder climbing; a perspectival path committed to a long obedience in the same direction; and a developmental approach to nurturing Jesus followers, rather than opening up another package of instant-discipleship cereal that might contain some fiber but little life-enriching nourishment. This book is a digestible feast, written by a guide who shares with us as a friend and sojourner. I already feel encouraged, more courageous, and eager to refocus on eternity. Thanks, Stacy, for sharing your life with us with such grace and love.

**Steve Hoke**
Director of Team Development, CRM

I have known Stacy Rinehart for decades. He is as consistent as anyone I've met. He stays the course. He is passionate about the Bible, following Jesus, and equipping others to be passionate about these same two things. In this book he reveals that his secret to being so consistent for a lifetime is to fix his eyes on what happens long after his lifetime. This is not just a theoretical illustration for Stacy. It is a lifestyle, and in this book he explains it so clearly that it can become a lifestyle for all of us as well.

Stacy Rinehart has spent his life teaching leaders in all walks of life and in nations around the globe what it means to follow Jesus. This book is the simplicity after the complexity—a sort of "Best of Stacy Rinehart Album." He takes over half a century of Bible reading, decades of conversations, years of sermons and curriculum, and months of writing and puts it all into a straightforward plan for application in real life.

I wish I had *Lead in Light of Eternity* when I started my journey as a follower of Christ. It would have kept me away from a lot of rabbit trails and side journeys that were full of promise and sounded like the answer but ended up being dead ends. I will suggest this book as a first read for those I know who are young in their faith. But this book is even more useful to those of us who have been on this journey a long time. It is one of the best character annual physicals I've ever seen, complete with encouragement to trim down, some uncomfortable moments, and a clear understanding of what must be changed if I want to be healthy for a lifetime and beyond.

**Brad Smith,**
President, Bakke Graduate University

Rare are writers who humbly challenge what appears successful but at a closer look fails to align with the values and vision of the kingdom of God. From time to time, we need to hear a prophetic voice call God's people, leaders and believers alike, to realign their life and leadership path in the way of Jesus. *Lead in Light of Eternity* will be a disturbing book, especially to those who have become comfortable in their leadership, who appear successful but give little attention to faithfully applying Jesus's perspective and practice. Others will find comfort that they are heading on the right track and find helpful principles and practices to pursue the eternal perspective now.

The book appears small in size and simple to read. However, if we read with an open heart and mind and let the Holy Spirit speak to us, we will be slowing down. We will take time to pause, ponder, examine, and evaluate where our life and leadership are in the light of eternity.

If we respond to the Holy Spirit's conviction, we have no choice but to repent and return to the right path. This will lead to spiritual renewal and make a difference to others.

Successful leaders promise to grow big churches and organizations that influence many people in their ministry network. But statistical count has never been a basis of spiritual success. In fact reliance on numbers or anything big and powerful has been a cause of God's disapproval that eventually leads to failure. Focusing on what appears big and successful is a temptation because all of us want the accolades of people. This book is subversive for global leaders who have accepted the secular-based leadership style. The author who has been involved in many international leadership-development events is very qualified to help us confront the disease of spectacular and success infecting global leaders today. The book calls all leaders to repentance, to deny self-centeredness, and to return to the example of Jesus.

The author is a mentor who guides his readers to focus on the heart, the very thing God looks at and where the Spirit works to change Christian leaders inside out. This book is indeed a good resource for mentoring leaders to be more like Jesus.

Leaders will find this book a landmark for developing spiritual leaders to live and lead like Jesus. I will make this a resource for mentoring conversation of thousands of pastors and ministry staff and leaders I guide to become spiritual leaders who are faithful to follow Jesus. Christian leaders must read this book to become prophetic in the way they live and lead.

### Herman A. Moldez

Herman is a coordinator of MentorLink International in the Philippines, working through the Philippine Council of Evangelical Churches. He facilitates spiritual peer mentoring of five thousand pastors.

# Dedication

This book is dedicated to our many colleagues, partners, prayer warriors, financial givers, and volunteers in the MentorLink network. You are truly a community of brothers and sisters who make a difference in the world. I admire your courage, faith, boldness, generosity, creativity, sacrifice, and wholehearted service to our Lord and His kingdom.

# Contents

# Foreword

Stacy Rinehart has uncovered the secret. Vital Christianity will never develop without leaders whom God provides to enable other members of the body of Christ to fulfill their mission of ministry.

This is a secret Jesus not only understood but also practiced. Throughout his ministry Jesus poured his life into his disciples, giving them an example to follow in coming generations. At times Jesus's approach to training leaders has been understood and his model followed. Too often "the church" has been confused with a mere institution, and the energy of those recognized as leaders has been dissipated as they focused on maintaining the organization rather than on transforming lives. Even the schools we look to as a source of biblical leaders to head our churches have failed significantly to recognize that Christ's church is a living organism, and that those who truly lead in Christ's church have little in common with the leaders of secular organizations.

Stacy recognizes this truth and has given much of his life to develop leaders who grasp the fact that we lead for eternity, not to gather a group of people who identify their congregation as "Reverend White's church." The goal of the leader must be a kingdom goal, one that nurtures obedience to Jesus, one that reaches out to draw men and women to Christ.

The reality is that if asked about their goals as leaders in Christ's church, most would vehemently deny that their goal is to carve out a group of followers, and insist that their intent is to draw men and women into personal relationships with Jesus and then to help them become all they can be as Jesus's followers. They would speak sincerely. The irony is that the way most go about ministry does not nurture obedience to Jesus, but it does encourage loyalty to an organization.

Given that those who lead our churches have the best of intentions, what has gone wrong? The answer is that we have not equipped individuals to be the kind of leader that Jesus was and that Jesus trained. In a nutshell this is what Stacy's book is about. It defines what leadership in the Body of Christ really is, and it shows how to train servant leaders who will reproduce themselves and introduce a fresh vitality into every dimension of the Christian experience.

I've known Stacy for many years now. I have observed his passion for nurturing leaders for Christ's church and his growing understanding of how true servant leaders are developed. I've had the privilege of working with him as he has developed tools to aid those who also catch the vision of producing leaders who are committed to the biblical model. This book distills all that Stacy has learned and is learning. It is a gift to the Church of inestimable value. As such I commend it to you as worthy of thought, soul searching, and prayer. May everyone who sees himself or herself as a leader take the teaching in this little book to heart.

Larry Richards, PhD

# Acknowledgments

This book has had many counselors and advisors. Some are notable in their contribution. Ralph Ennis, my longtime friend, made strategic suggestions and was always available to interact with me about any issue I faced with this book. Ole Gulbrandsen went above and beyond in his thorough and invaluable comments on each chapter. My wife, Paula, a seasoned author, made wise editorial suggestions. Christine Weddle lent her amazing talent in some of the details of publication and other administrative tasks. Larry Thompson of Gravitation Studios gave his heart and talent in the book-cover design. There are a number of readers who labored with me in the writing process and gave invaluable feedback. Finally, I want to thank those who gave of their heart and time to read the manuscript and write an endorsement—you can see who they are in the front of this book.

What is written in this book comes out of my life, study, and experiences, but I don't know where I would be without the mentors the Lord provided in years past. Gordon VanAmburgh, Chet Steffey, Elliott Johnson, Ron Blue, Jim White, John Crawford, Skip Gray, Donald McGilchrist, Jim Petersen, Paul Stanley, and Terry Taylor are all men who made significant contributions to my life. They showed patience, wisdom, and grace as I questioned and processed life, ministry, and leadership issues with them. Thank you. I stand on your shoulders.

The Lord has given some amazing peer mentors who counsel and encourage me in this stage of life. We help each other in our walk of faith. They are an encouragement to me to finish the journey strong. I look forward to what the Lord has ahead for us in our fellowship.

# Introduction

"Long ago, at many times and in many ways, God spoke to our fathers by the prophets, but in these last days he has spoken to us by his Son, whom he appointed the heir of all things, through whom also he created the world. He is the radiance of the glory of God and the exact imprint of his nature, and he upholds the universe by the word of his power" (Heb. 1:1–3).

This book is about Jesus and leading in His kingdom. He has much to say to each of us who lead or want to lead and influence people.

I have five goals in writing this book:

1. Encourage you to be a successful leader in Jesus's kingdom so that when you stand before Him, you will hear, "Well done, good and faithful servant"
2. Share some of my own journey in leadership, including ups and downs
3. Point you to Jesus, who will evaluate your life and leadership, motives, values, heart, and character and how you treated and developed people
4. Remind you of what Jesus wants and what He rebukes or rejects among kingdom leaders
5. Envision you in the importance of leading from the inside out and multiplying Christlike leaders

## Who is the book for?

This book is for ministry leaders, including pastors; deacons; elders; Bible-study leaders; house-church leaders; funders of ministries and churches; denominational leaders; network leaders; business owners; professionals; supervisors; team leaders; missionaries; Bible teachers; mission-organization leaders; homemakers; church planters; seminary and Bible-college students; staff and faculty; and anyone who aspires to live and lead like Jesus in the workplace, the church, the mission field, or the world.

**All author royalties go to fund Christlike leaders who multiply Christlike leaders.** I count it a privilege to serve as a guide through this book. My joy is to make it available to as many as possible. Paperback and Kindle versions are available from Amazon.com. All royalties go to a special account in MentorLink International, dedicated to help fund leaders and ministries in the developing world who are focused on multiplying Christlike leaders. For my brothers and sisters who cannot afford to purchase a copy or do not have a way to acquire the book through Amazon.com, it is available as a free PDF download from www. MentorLink.org.

Let's begin our journey together.

Stacy T. Rinehart
Founder, MentorLink International

# Chapter 1

*So teach us to number our days that we may
present to Thee a heart of wisdom.*

PSALM 90:12

On a clear day, the Grand Canyon seen at thirty-five thousand feet presents a spectacular sight. Deep canyon walls a mile higher than the river below make a beautiful canvas of colors, shades of brown, blue, green, and tan. It is indescribable beauty, begging to be viewed firsthand.

Only about a one thousand people a year, though, are granted permits to raft down the actual river at the bottom of this great gorge. My son and I took the father-son trip of a lifetime, happy for the privilege to fight the rapids and camp beside the river. As our plane descended, we had visions of Indiana Jones on steroids, two men heroically battling the elements, victory assured.

That was all before the predeparture orientation. This was not going to be a Boy Scout canoe trip. Scorpions, rattlesnakes, and wandering off alone were hazards that could mean life or death. Should you get thrown overboard, feetfirst is the only way to travel downstream. The mere report of canyon temperature (routinely above 110 degrees, or 43 degrees Celsius) was enough to make me sweat. I had to do some serious grappling with the reality that I would climb 4,380 feet (1,334 meters) straight up, in 9.5 miles (15.3 kilometers) at the end of our trip.

I was glad I'd seen the big view from the sky.

We arrived at the river and loaded into our raft with our guide. The guide's role was to steer the raft, keep us safe, and tell us when to paddle forward or in reverse. Our guide was the one person who knew the river and had perspective on the rapids and how to safely navigate the dangers.

The float down the river started out so peacefully I could have taken a nap. That lasted about an hour. Then came the first rapid and that was the last I saw of peaceful. The next one hundred miles were packed with many extremely dangerous rapids.

It was just like the movies: a deafening roar of water as waves crashed against massive boulders, foam and spray everywhere. This was battling the elements, all right, but I didn't feel so victorious.

Leadership in the kingdom of God is much like this raft trip. It's the big-picture view that will keep us moving forward, facing the rapids of opposition or sinful pride or our own nagging sense of inadequacy. Without perspective, we may not be able to get down that river well— or guide and shepherd others.

We are living in a time when it's particularly hard to get a perspective on leading God's people in a way Jesus would recognize. The clamor is for big numbers and quick results. Offering a cup of cold water to the least of these does not build a reputation for success, not in this current climate. The pressure is to be the hero, the strong leader who won't take "no," or the guy who's boss.

Where is our faith in the power of the Gospel, rather than sheer human effort?

Much like my Grand Canyon trip, we can begin this journey of being a leader—a Christian leader—with the best of intentions and high ideals, but this does not sustain. When the going gets rough, we will feel swamped, and the tendency is to do what comes naturally: dominate and control, go with the flow of what other leaders around us do. We will strive to be the hero, the focus of people's attention, and the leader of a vibrant ministry organization or church.

"Jesus, for the joy set before Him, endured the cross…" the writer of Hebrews said. In other words, this big-picture view of eternity with the Father and hearing Him say, "Well done," was the motivation and the prize. *Even for Christ.* Some people call this an "eternal perspective." It's not unlike that beautiful big-picture view of the Grand Canyon that kept me paddling and hiking up a canyon wall. The reality that we will stand before Jesus Christ, the King of Kings and Lord of Lords, shapes our perspective on what it means to lead as Christ led.

Before I became a Christ follower, the idea of leading—and leading well—captivated me. As a manager I was trained to think in terms of an even wider variety of accomplishments. In the military I learned to measure success by position. But when I read the life of Jesus and began to follow Him, God turned many of those ideas upside down.

## My Early Understanding of Leadership
I always had a sense of awe and wonder when I saw how sensitively Jesus responded to those in need or how directly He confronted hypocrisy. He was marching to no one else's drummer. When we watch Him raise

the dead or see His humility before His accusers, all we can do is offer Him praise, leave our fishing boat by the sea, and follow.

What I saw of Christ also produced something of a war inside me. At the tender age of nineteen, I became an assistant manager in one of the busiest McDonald's in Southern California. Ray Kroc, McDonald's legendary founder, often stopped by our store on the way to his ranch. I admired his expensive suits, Rolls Royce, and confident demeanor. I had visions of becoming a version of an entrepreneur like him.

I was rolling along on my own little conveyor belt of achieving-something-in-life until one day, I opened the mailbox to discover a letter from President Richard Nixon. He invited me to take a free physical exam! I knew what that meant. The Vietnam War was in full swing, and I was set to be drafted into the army. Rather than be forced to be a private, I enlisted to go to officer candidate school.

Whether it was a military environment or a business one, the values were and are much the same: rise to the top, promote yourself, and accumulate the prizes.

One day at Fort Benning, Georgia, I joined a pickup football game with a group of guys. They played decent football. The thing that struck me as odd was that they didn't swear. When the game was over, they invited me to some sort of gathering that seemed vaguely Christian, so I did what any normal guy would do. I went to a movie and showed up in time for dessert. A helicopter pilot spotted me right away as the new guy in the room. He shared the simplicity of the Gospel with me, and given that the prospect of death on a battlefield in Vietnam had sharpened my listening skills, he had my attention. I listened. I heard. I believed.

From my earliest days of following Christ, I sensed that He would turn what it meant to be a leader upside down and inside out. In both concept and practice, He intended to put me on a different path with a different definition of being a leader. He rattled me to the core.

## The Dot and the Line

Perhaps the simplest and clearest way I can describe this change in perspective that Jesus brings is by the illustration of "the dot and the line." It's really a picture of a radically different way to see your life and what it means.

The line represents the unending nature of eternity. The dot on the line is my single, solitary life in space and time.

One of the great temptations of our lives is to live for the here and now—to live for the dot. What we can see, feel, taste, and touch, as though this life was all there is—we call this a 'temporal perspective'. But eternity is forever. What is amazing is that we can do things in this life that have an eternal impact and bear fruit that lasts forever. We can invest in eternal treasures and gain rewards that are everlasting. This is an "eternal perspective."

Consider the simple example of Christ's teaching about giving to the poor: "Do not sound a trumpet before you as the hypocrites do in the synagogues and in the streets, so that they may be honored by men (Matt. 6:2)." No longer could a person give to the poor in order to be honored by men. If we live for the temporal, for the world's acclaim, then Christ says that we have our reward in full. If we live for the "dot," then all we have is the "dot," so to speak.

> *What is amazing is that we can do things in this life that have an eternal impact and bear fruit that lasts forever.*

5

What really matters *there* informs what matters *here*. None of our trinkets and toys will survive. But the people of God around the throne of the Lamb, His kingdom come, this will fill the picture forever.

The world around us only thinks and acts for the here and now. Jesus taught His followers to reverse this emphasis. That's one part of what makes His Gospel so radical. And it's at the heart of what makes leadership in His Body different than leadership in a corporation.

If we orient our heart, mind, values, and treatment of others by an eternal perspective, then our reward is also an eternal one.

> *Jesus calls us to let loose our grip on the temporal. He calls us to resist the temptation to lead like the world or measure our ministry success by the criteria of the culture we live in.*

Something of that heart and the actions that stem from it actually remains for eternity. What an amazing thought! Would any of us really want to live for the accolades of the here and now if we really grasp the larger picture?

Jesus calls us to let loose our grip on the temporal. He calls us to resist the temptation to lead like the world or measure our ministry success by the criteria of the culture we live in.

James compared our lives to a vapor that appears for a little while and then vanishes (James 4:14). It's not a terribly complimentary picture. Sometimes I sober myself by breathing on a cold window pane and watching how quickly that breath evaporates.

Then I turn to the encouragement that Jesus offers when we lift our eyes to eternity. He says what is done in secret in His name will be rewarded no matter how small. "Well done good and faithful servant" is the praise that awaits us.

He calls us to serve Him and His kingdom purposes. He calls us to give ourselves to something far bigger and more important than our own agenda and fleshly desires.

When we live and lead with an eternal perspective, we acknowledge that life is short. We will soon pass from this life and enter into His presence for all eternity. Sometimes our Christ-centered choices are difficult. "We look not at the things which are seen, but at the things which are not seen; for the things which are seen are temporal, but the things which are not seen are eternal," Paul says (2 Cor. 17–18).

The rewards of this life are of little importance when compared to the rewards stored up in eternity. These are rewards given by Him for what we did on His behalf—our sacrifices, faithfulness, obedience, integrity, giving, prayers, and character. He gives rewards for how we lead others in His kingdom, how we treat people and how we faithfully represent Him.

For many of us, living for the line will mean reorientating what we strive to accomplish in our ministries, what we strive to do with our work, what we consider important, and whom we seek to please and serve. The issue is success in Jesus's eyes, not success in the world's.

## A Look Ahead
In the pages that follow, we unfold the theme of leading in light of eternity. For now, here is a brief summary of each chapter. Each of us will be audited by Jesus—we are accountable to Him (chapter 2). We each have to choose whether we will lead in the natural ways of the flesh or follow Jesus's ways (chapter 3). Jesus calls us to lead from the inside out, focusing on our heart, character, values, and motives (chapter 4). We look at

the Leader's Covenant as "aspirations" for living and leading like Christ (chapter 5). We delve into the principles of how Jesus took common people and made them into world-changing leaders (chapter 6). There is a subject we just don't want to talk about—false leaders—but we will (chapter 7). Like the polluted air in Beijing, we are at spiritual risk with the idolatry of organizationalism (chapter 8). Then we summarize this book with seven realities of the kingdom (chapter 9).

## Prayer
*Lord, grant me grace and insight to see things more from your perspective and to value them as you do and to live and lead in light of eternity. (2 Cor. 4:17–18)*

## Questions for Thought or Discussion
1. What things in my life and ministry reveal that I am leading for the here and now?
2. What are some action steps I can take to lead in light of eternity?
3. "We who are ministry leaders are like the river guides." What three to five things reveal that I am working to lead others in the right direction?

# Chapter 2

## Lead with Accountability in Mind

Google Maps is amazing GPS technology available right on our mobile phones. We put in a destination; it determines where we are and plots several possible routes to get us there. It shows which is fastest, how long each route will take, and the distance traveled. It tells us if there are toll roads or back roads in each route. Then we pick one and follow its directions.

If we make a decision to alter the route, it compensates and tells us where to turn in order to head toward our destination. Many of us have come to rely on it when in a strange place. It is marvelous technology.

In life most of us know the final destination. Even if we don't know the destination, we are headed there. The destination for each of us is standing before Jesus. There are many routes each of us could take. Often we deviate from His route, and yet in His love, grace, and kindness, like the GPS, He redirects us and points us in the right direction. We can ignore His directions and go our own way, but we have no choice about the destination.

*When* we arrive at the destination is not our choice. Just a few minutes ago, I heard that a friend had a terrible bicycle accident and was killed. I am saddened by this news. When he went on his bike ride yesterday afternoon, he did not plan to stand before Jesus that evening. Yet right now as I write, he is in Jesus's presence. In this life, he made significant contributions to the kingdom and Jesus's work in the lives of many. He helped form a ministry that now has a national reach.

## Will Jesus Say, "Well Done"?

When I stand before Jesus, His praise, "Well done, good and faithful servant" is what I want to hear. Just because I am a Christian and a leader does not mean that is what I will hear. How I lead, how I treat people, the motives I have, the intent of my heart, and how I develop people are all aspects of how He will evaluate me.

Paul says it this way:

> I am conscious of nothing against myself, yet I am not by this acquitted; but the one who examines me is the Lord. Therefore do not go on passing judgment before the time, but wait until the Lord comes who will both bring to light the things hidden in the darkness and disclose the motives of men's hearts; and then each man's praise will come from God. (1 Cor. 4:4–5)

I've been watching, studying and working among leaders now for over four decades. During this time I've had leadership roles in churches, mission boards, ministry networks, large ministries, and small ministries. Some I started, some I inherited, and some I joined. In the last twenty-five years, my focus has been outside the United States while still living in the United States and traveling. In all of this, I have one observation: many ministry leaders seem to operate as though they are not accountable to Jesus.

There seems to be a pervasive ignorance of Jesus's standards, evaluation criteria, and mandates for those who lead His people. Yet, someday, each of us will stand before Him to give an account. Then we all will know, and our opportunity to be the person the Lord would have us be will have passed. Further, we collectively seem to ignore the teachings and pattern of Jesus and His apostles about kingdom leadership and its context. (Note: I expand this in my book *Upside Down*. For a simple overview see Appendix B and C.)

Every year our mission conducts an audit of our finances. This serves several purposes. We must report our financials to the US government, and we need to report our finances and ministry results to our donors in the form of an annual report. We hire an accounting firm to conduct the audit, provide a summary report, and submit the required government forms. We pay their fees, and the process is repeated again the next year. Each year we pray and plan for improvements and new growth.

> *Each of us will have only one audit before Jesus—this is the final audit. Leading in light of eternity is leading with this in mind.*

Each of us will have only one audit before Jesus—this is the final audit. Leading in light of eternity is leading with this in mind. The destination is clear. The fact that Jesus will audit me orients how I lead, live, and minister in this life. It informs me of what I value as a leader, how I spend my time, and what is acceptable for me to do or not do.

It is easy to confuse Jesus's grace, love, and forgiveness with a lack of accountability to Him. Jesus is loving, forgiving, gracious, and merciful. He is our Great High Priest interceding on our behalf before the throne.

At the same time, He is the Righteous Judge and will evaluate and reward our faithfulness. Both are true.

## It's All about the Destination

How do you take common working-class young people and make them true Christlike leaders? How do you take people who live for all kinds of selfish reasons and mold them into sacrificial leaders? How do you take people who only know how to use financial, positional, or social power to accomplish their purposes and turn them into people who use the power of being a servant? How do you take people who live by religious activity and obligations and turn them into people who live for Jesus? How do you take people bound by the perspective of the here and now and make them into world-changing people who live with the end in mind?

How? Jesus shows us how.

Most of us live as though this life is all there is. Yes, heaven is in our future, but is that all there is? Jesus focused the twelve on realities of the future and the fact that they will be evaluated and rewarded. Jesus taught that rewards are a significant motivation.

Esteem and accolades are rewards for those who practice their righteousness to be noticed by people. Those who seek this reward have no reward from the Father (Matt. 6:1). Leaders, financial givers, and prayers who live to be honored by others have their reward in full in this life. But those who know that the Father sees what is done in secret operate differently. They lead, live, give, and pray with the end in mind, knowing that One really knows what is going on in their hearts.

## Treasures

Treasures are things of value that people seek. They can be bought or sold on the open market. People pour money into the stock market, seeking growth of their treasures. The Dow has gone up 31 percent in the last two and a half years.

Treasures are also things like houses and collectibles (antique cars, coins, art, sports memorabilia, etc.) that appreciate in value and can be sold later at a profit. But there is no certainty. Think of the global financial crisis of 2008. Think of the collapse of the housing market at the same time. Even today, many still live in houses that they owe more on than what they are worth. In this life there is no certainty when it comes to treasures. Gold, stocks, collectibles, and houses are all subject to thieves or destruction. But Jesus says, lay up for yourselves treasures in heaven, where they can't be stolen or destroyed.

Moses understood this. He was the prince of the land. As a son of Pharaoh's daughter, he had all the wealth, prestige, power, and privileges anyone could want. Only Pharaoh had more. He had the best training, education, and facilities available in the world at the time. Treasures, pleasures, and perks were all his. Yet he turned away from it all.

Why did he do this? What motivated him? Why did he choose to take up the cause of the slave caste and identify with them? Why did he endure ill treatment rather than enjoy the "passing pleasures" of his lifestyle as royalty? He knew he was accountable. He considered "the reproach of Christ greater riches than the treasures of Egypt; for he was looking forward to the reward" (Heb. 11:26).

When we think of treasures, rewards, and being audited by Jesus, it is easy to pass off these ideas we tuck into the back of our minds. But consider who spoke these truths. Seems to me we will be wise to elevate our understanding of who Jesus is.

**Who Is Jesus?**
I had the privilege of sharing the homily at my mother-in-law's funeral. Her name was Polly and in many ways she was an amazing woman. This took place on my thirty-ninth wedding anniversary. It was the same church but only a few of the same people. As I pondered what to say, it occurred to me that in times like these, we really want to look to Jesus

for hope and consolation. Yet Jesus is often just a name used by those in need.

I thought the best thing I could do was paint the context of who Jesus is so that when I talked about Jesus's words of comfort, there was more meaning and perhaps understanding.

I began the homily by stating, "Thirty-nine years ago today, Polly was the mother of the bride in this church when Paula and I married." I shared a few other comments and then said, "My goal is to bring our focus on Jesus, who is our hope. How do we focus on Jesus in just a few minutes? His names! His names reflect who He is. Listen to some of His names." Then I read them slowly.

| | |
|---|---|
| Almighty God | Lamb of God |
| Alpha and Omega | Light of the World |
| Ancient of Days | Living Brea |
| Anointed One | Living Water |
| Beginning and the Ending | Lord of All |
| Beloved Son | Lord of Hosts |
| Bread of Life | Lord of Lords |
| Bridegroom | Mediator |
| Bright and Morning Star | Messiah |
| Captain of Our Salvation | Mighty God |
| Christ | Most High God |
| Creator of All Things | Only Begotten Son |
| Deliverer | Power of God |
| Eternal God | Prince of Peace |
| Eternal Judge | Redeemer |
| Faithful and True | Resurrection and the Life |
| First and the Last | Righteous Judge |
| God of the Whole Earth | Rock, the |
| God's Anointed | Savior |
| Good Shepherd | Shepherd |

| | |
|---|---|
| Heir of All Things | Son of God |
| Holy One | Son of the Living God |
| King of Kings | Word of Life |

I continued. "Who Jesus is makes all the difference when He says something. It is in this context that I share words of hope. Jesus says, 'In My Father's house are many dwelling places; if it were not so, I would have told you; for I go to prepare a place for you. If I go and prepare a place for you, I will come again and receive you to Myself, that where I am, there you may be also' (John 14: 2–3). Jesus's words have meaning because of Who He is."

"Jesus Christ is Lord" seems so simple, so commonplace. We sing about Jesus as Lord, teach it, pray it, and yet do we stop to really ponder what this means to us who are leaders among His people? Does this reality shape how we lead?

As Lord, He is the one we work for. He is the one who will evaluate us and our ministries. These are not just words on paper but rather ultimate reality.

When I work for a company, I am responsible to do my job, please my boss, and accomplish the tasks and responsibilities assigned to me. Periodically, I face a performance review, which reveals how I am doing and how I can improve.

Ultimately, I will be evaluated by Jesus when I stand before Him to receive His praise. My life and ministry will be over. What I did or didn't do will be apparent. How I treated people will be clear. What my motives were and things I did in secret will become known and evaluated. How I developed people to serve in His kingdom will be compared to His example and teachings.

Why wait till then? Like any good employee, the goal is to find out as soon as possible what the company's and boss's expectations are and meet them. Promotions and raises often follow outstanding reviews. In a similar way, we can dig into Jesus's teaching to understand what He expects and values.

He made it clear what He expects from those who lead in His kingdom. He reveals what He values, what motivations please Him, and what attitudes He expects from His servants. He has shown and taught us how to lead in His kingdom and how to treat those we serve. He modeled how to develop people.

Notice I didn't say, read books, listen to lectures, or follow some ministry leader and do what he or she says. However, in order to grasp Jesus's teachings and model, these may be helpful. When you and I stand before Jesus, He will evaluate us on what He taught and modeled. He is Lord. Frankly it really doesn't matter what I say about leading in His kingdom, or what anyone else says. The only one that counts is Jesus. "And there is no creature hidden from His sight, but all things are open and laid bare to the eyes of Him with whom we have to do" (Heb. 4:13).

## Legacy Thinking

There is a popular notion that we must give attention to our "legacy"—that is, what we leave behind in this life. This notion means, "I want people to think well of me when I am gone." Notice, the emphasis is what people think of me, what my reputation is, and what I leave behind that people see or influences how they feel about me. Here is the question: can this emphasis steer me toward living for the dot, or does it steer me toward living for the line?

The issue of legacy, eternal legacy, is not settled in the world's eyes but rather in Jesus's. Stewarding one's life for the glory of God may leave behind a "legacy" that people value in the here and now, but the greater priority is to steward our life so that we are rewarded by Jesus's words, "Well done, good and faithful servant." The evaluation of a leader in

Jesus's kingdom is different from what the world values. "God sees not as man sees, for man looks at the outward appearance but the Lord looks at the heart" (1 Sam. 16:7). Successful Christian leaders and successful Christians are those who are successful in Jesus's eyes.

## My Goal

I want to guide you toward becoming an authentic leader in Jesus's kingdom. My role in writing this book is to point you to Jesus to understand and practice leadership in His kingdom. My ultimate goal is to sharpen your focus and leadership practices to reflect Jesus's ways, values, and priorities. I, too, will stand before Him to give an account.

Many books, conferences, and seminars on ministry leadership reflect the author's or speaker's model of "success." The underlying message is, "If you practice these things, you can be just like me and be a success, too." Many big-name ministry leaders seem to be saying, "Get out of the way, Jesus, and let me show You how to lead and do ministry." Jesus's way and mandates are at best an afterthought to them. Success in ministry is often defined as what can be seen and measured. This is faulty because many who live for what can be counted "receive their reward in full" in this life.

> *Many "big name" ministry leaders seem to be saying, "Get out of the way, Jesus, and let me show You how to lead and do ministry." Jesus's way and mandates are at best an afterthought to them.*

If you want to know what success is in Jesus's kingdom, study Him as written in the New Testament. If you want to know what pleases Him, follow His ways. If you want to avoid His rebuke, understand what or who He rebuked in His ministry and avoid their ways. It is not complex. The body of knowledge is not significant.

My role, like the GPS on my mobile phone, is to help you focus on the destination and to reroute you if you have strayed. To be personally open, I have regular new insights into my own wanderings from Christlike leadership. This brings me to repentance. Repentance is a sign that the Holy Spirit is teaching and convicting me. This is good! I hope you have many times of confession and repentance as you read this book.

## Final Assessment

Each of us will stand individually before Jesus. Just to be clear, I say again, this is not a salvation evaluation but rather a faithfulness review. Each of us will give an account. "For we must all appear before the judgment seat of Christ, so that each one may be recompensed for his deeds in the body, according to what he has done, whether good or bad" (2 Cor. 5:10). This judgment seat is only for believers.

In this evaluation we are before the Lord. Those in Christ have a sure eternal future. Our names are written in the Book of Life (Rev. 20:12–15). Those who are not in Christ face a devastating future away from Jesus and the presence of His glory (2 Thess. 1:6–10). Those not in Christ will be evaluated by their deeds where records are kept in the "books" (Rev. 20:12–15). The eternal suffering and anguish for those who refuse Jesus cannot be described. This is not short-term suffering like we might picture as torture; it is long term—as in forever and ever. Eternity is a long time.

At Christ's judgment seat, our works, values, motives, what we've done in secret, how we treated people, and how we developed people will all be evaluated.

> Now if any man builds on the foundation with gold, silver, precious stones, wood, hay, straw, each man's work

will become evident; for the day will show it because it is to be revealed with fire, and the fire itself will test the quality of each man's work. If any man's work which he has built on it remains, he will receive a reward. If any man's work is burned up, he will suffer loss; but he himself will be saved, yet so as through fire. (1 Cor. 3:12–15)

This is a faithfulness evaluation. Some will have little left after the evaluation, but they will still be "saved, yet as through fire." Each person's work will be evident. Some of what I do in life and ministry is wood, hay, and stubble and will be burned up. Some of what I do is gold, silver, and precious stones and will remain. It is what remains, having stood the evaluation of Jesus, that I will be rewarded.

Imagine leaders of large ministries or churches with little to show for it after the evaluation because they operated their ministry in the flesh, and while speaking God words, they used fleshly strategies, personal charisma, human wisdom, and worldly tools to lead. Imagine people who faithfully attended church, did all kinds of church activities, and carried all kinds of church responsibilities and after the evaluation have little to show for it.

On the other hand, imagine the janitor of a hospital, who worked for years cleaning up other people's messes, having much reward because the janitor did what he or she did for Jesus. Jesus will reward his or her faithfulness, motives, humility, and spiritual responses to humiliating events. Imagine a church planter or missionary who lived faithfully, laboring among a Muslim people group, seeing few results in terms of converts or even a church planted, having more reward than the president of a mission organization. Imagine a pastor of a rural or urban church with less than one hundred members having more reward than the megachurch pastor with large media attention, books written, and high honorariums for speaking engagements. This will happen.

We are not saying that leading large ministries and faithfully serving a church or ministry are wrong. Nor are we saying that small is better. We are only pointing out that what man esteems is of little importance to Jesus. He looks at the heart, motives, actions, values, character, and strategies.

For some, they do their actions to be noticed. Jesus says, "They have their reward in full." In this life there are rewards. We know what they are in our contexts, and we strive for them. Rewards given us after our evaluation before Jesus are given based on Jesus Christ's criteria.

Leaders in His kingdom should know this. Jesus and His apostles taught about good and bad leaders. In fact, false leaders are addressed in each book of the New Testament except Philemon and James. This is an important fact, and we will delve into this in chapter 7. Leaders are accountable to Jesus for their activities, responses, faithfulness, and how they treat and develop people.

The truly wise and faithful leader in His kingdom leads with the mindset that he is accountable to the Lord of Lords. Jesus says, "Behold, I am coming quickly, and My reward is with Me, to render to every man according to what he has done" (Rev. 22:12).

**Prayer**
*Lord Jesus, I want to honor you with my heart, motives, values and character and in the ways I lead and serve people. Thank you that you have called me into your service.* (Heb. 4:13)

**Questions for Thought or Discussion**
1. How does the reality of Jesus's Lordship affect your understanding and responsibilities in leading and influencing others?

2. What are some ways that you can help other leaders more align themselves with Jesus?
3. What is the Spirit saying to you from this chapter? From the book so far?

# Chapter 3

## Moving from Left to Right

became a follower of Jesus in December of 1970. Something had changed when I returned to my bachelor officer's quarters that evening. I went expecting a party and came home a changed man. In the weeks and months following, many came to help me grow and understand what happened. They showed me how to live for Jesus, learn from Him, and help others do the same. This is called follow-up. My growth in Christ would have floundered without it.

We look at orphanages, abused children, or child trafficking and know it is a personal tragedy for each child affected. No one is there to care for, nourish, and love each child. Their growth is limited, perhaps retarded. In a similar way, think of the spiritual children coming to Jesus with no one to help them learn to walk with Him, pray, read their Bibles, or so many other basic things received when we are adopted into the Father's family by His amazing grace and mercy. Just because a person is a new Christian does not mean he or she knows how to walk with Jesus.

The flesh (our sinful nature) is our natural default way of operating. As we mature in Christ, we can move away from spiritual immaturity and move toward godliness of life, character, and relationships.

Likewise, there is a fleshly, natural way to lead. Just because a person is a Christian and a leader does not mean he or she operates according to Jesus's ways. We have to be continually transformed into the ways of leading in Jesus's kingdom. A new Christian has to grow, mature, and learn the ways of walking with Jesus. Growing into leading like Jesus is the same. To learn the ways of Jesus is a process that takes time and constant focus.

Deep fleshly issues confront leaders. They are motives, values, character, and heart issues that if not addressed can lead to failure. No matter what we say or what our doctrine, gifts, or charisma is, our flesh can undermine the very ministry and people we attempt to serve in Jesus's name.

We in MentorLink call these the Transformational Value Shifts. These shifts were articulated by a small international group of leaders in 2001. They have been refined over the years, have received input from leaders in over fifty nations, and have been validated as core issues by leaders wherever we have explained them.

Here's the bottom line: we ministry leaders tend to operate in the flesh because it feels so natural. We esteem other ministry leaders who operate in the same way. However, we must learn to turn away from fleshly ways of leading and move to the ways of the Spirit. Here's the catch—the issues are almost always issues of the heart, values, character, and motives. The goal is to move from left to right.

# Transformational Value Shifts

**Leaving behind leadership values and practices of the flesh**

**Pursuing leadership values and practices of the Spirit**

| | |
|---|---|
| **BUILDING MY EMPIRE**<br><br>Believing and acting as if God is primarily at work in the world through me, my ministry, or my organization; believing and acting independently of other Christians as if they are "less important." | **BUILDING GOD'S KINGDOM**<br><br>Having a personal and holistic understanding of the kingdom of God and a perspective that seeks the glory of Christ and the promotion of His Kingdom worldwide. |
| **ENVIRONMENTS OF CONTROL**<br><br>Living and leading in a performance-based or controlling environment which can produce competitiveness, critical attitudes, self-righteous pride and/or burnout. | **ENVIRONMENTS OF GRACE**<br><br>Leadership based on the finished work of Christ; living and leading in humility, openness, and love; treating others with acceptance, forgiveness, honesty, and embracing accountability. |
| **POWER-BASED LEADERSHIP**<br><br>Leading primarily through position, power, and political influence; often relying on manipulation or organizational authority; a lack of trust and of empowering of others. | **SERVANT LEADERSHIP**<br><br>Leading and influencing others through authentic relationships, integrity, and service; giving oneself to meet the needs of others and empowering them to succeed. |
| **ELISTISM AND SELF-SUFFICIENCY**<br><br>Attempting to be personally competent in every area of leadership responsibility; living as a stressed and relationally distant leader; difficulty working together as part of the Body. | **COLLABORATION AND COMMUNITY**<br><br>Leading as part of a team that cooperates together to carry out God's work; influencing through relationships, mutual accountability, delegation, and the empowerment of others. |
| **ACCIDENTALLY ADDING OTHER LEADERS**<br><br>Small and inadequate numbers of leaders are developed through a reliance primarily on formal or formulaic programs. This is rooted in a focus on the *quantitative* (numbers and visible results). | **INTENTIONALLY MULTIPLYING LEADERS**<br><br>Multiplying leadership growth through the mentoring of gifted, reproducing leaders whose hearts' desire and commitment is to humbly and strategically expand God's kingdom (*qualitative*). |

We share a version of this overview in a seminar we call "Passing It On." When leaders see this, most of them know in their hearts they are right. They want to operate on the right side of the chart, but they also know how easy and natural it is to fall back to the left side.

Appendix A is a personal assessment of each value shift developed and refined over many years and nations as part of the "Passing It On" manual. It's a tool designed to bring each value shift down to every leader's real world. Most are not operating completely in the flesh or in the spirit, but rather somewhere between. The scale allows us to see where we are. As you go through each value shift, take a minute to rate yourself with a number from one (operating in the flesh) to ten (operating in the Spirit).

We were in India conducting a "Passing It On" seminar when one leader said, "I was all ones before the seminar, and after the seminar I am all tens." We appreciated his enthusiasm but assured him that it doesn't work that way. One does not make that radical a shift in just a few days. Just knowing the right answers does not mean one's life has changed.

Let's look at each one of these in some detail.

## Value Shift 1
## From "Building My Empire" to "Building God's Kingdom"

I am saddened every time I think about Diotrephes. He was a man we would all recognize—ambitious, driven, in charge, domineering, and commanding attention. He thought he had it all together. He thought he had God's favor because his ministry was large and growing. He was a prominent leader.

The apostle John, the one whom Jesus loved, wrote to Gaius about the issues.

I wrote to the church, but Diotrephes, who loves to be first, will have nothing to do with us. So if I come, I will call attention to what he is doing, gossiping maliciously about us. Not satisfied with that, he refuses to welcome the brothers. He also stops those who want to do so and puts them out of the church. Dear friend, do not imitate what is evil but what is good. (3 John 9–11)

Diotrephes was driven to be first—so much so that he didn't want anything to do with John. Can you imagine not inviting the apostle John to speak?

In my early thirties, I remember meeting Dr. J. Oswald Sanders, past president of China Inland Mission and author of many books, including *Spiritual Leadership* (Moody Press, 1967). I sat with him at a meal after listening to him teach. My heart was moved just sitting beside him. He was in his nineties at the time and still zealous for the things of God. I was young but knew I wanted to be like him in some way. The apostle John was even more of a privilege to be around. He knew the Lord first-hand. He was probably the only living one of the original twelve.

But Diotrephes wanted to be the star. He wanted the spotlight—the focus of attention. John was a challenge, a threat.

Everywhere I speak to pastors and ministry leaders, I raise the example of Diotrephes and gave the instruction, "Compare and contrast Diotrephes with ministry leaders and pastors in your part of the world." They give me a blank stare—many look down. I then break them into small groups to discuss Diotrephes's model of ministry leadership.

What Diotrephes did feels right to our flesh. It seems so natural. A leader can look wildly successful yet have Diotrephes's heart. We are called to repent from leading in the flesh and lead by reliance upon the Spirit.

There is another leader worth remembering. He put others first even over his own interests. Paul spoke highly of him.

> I hope in the Lord Jesus to send Timothy to you soon, that I also may be cheered when I receive news about you. I have no one else like him, who takes a genuine interest in your welfare. For everyone looks out for his own interests, not those of Christ Jesus. (Philippians 2:19–21)

What is the difference between Diotrephes and Timothy? One operates in the flesh building his own empire. The other operates in the Spirit, counting others as more important than himself.

In our day which one of these two would be more esteemed? Many would say Diotrephes because of his strong leadership. In Jesus's eyes which one will be rewarded? Which one was leading in light of eternity?

*Summary:* A leader who is being transformed by Jesus Christ is one… whose focus is changing from building his own empire—promoting himself, his ministry, or his organization—to building the kingdom of God—seeking the glory of Christ and the promotion of God's kingdom in a way that touches every area of life, ministry, and culture.

*Reminder:* Assess yourself with the tool provided in Appendix A.

## Value Shift 2
## From "Environments of Control" to "Environments of Grace"

Jesus did not confront any group of people in His teachings except the class of religious leaders—the scribes and Pharisees. "Woe to you scribes and Pharisees, hypocrites!" Multiple times Jesus repeats this (Matt. 23). I certainly don't want the Lord to say this about me. The scribes and

Pharisees said one thing and did another. They controlled people by using religious rules and regulations while at the same time ignoring the real issues of the heart. They used their position as experts in the law to subject people to their control—often for their selfish benefit.

> Woe to you, scribes and Pharisees, hypocrites! For you tithe mint and dill and cumin, and have neglected the weightier provisions of the law: justice and mercy and faithfulness; but these are the things you should have done without neglecting the others. You blind guides, who strain out a gnat and swallow a camel! (Matt. 23:23–24)

> Woe to you, scribes and Pharisees, hypocrites! For you clean the outside of the cup and of the dish, but inside they are full of robbery and self-indulgence. You blind Pharisee, first clean the inside of the cup and of the dish, so that the outside of it may become clean also. (Matt. 23:25–26)

> Woe to you, scribes and Pharisees, hypocrites! For you are like whitewashed tombs which on the outside appear beautiful, but inside they are full of dead men's bones and all uncleanness. So you, too, outwardly appear righteous to men, but inwardly you are full of hypocrisy and lawlessness. (Matt. 23:27–28)

It is not unusual to find that the very places where the Gospel is advancing the issues of legalism and control surface because the new growth and initiatives to win people to Christ threaten leaders.

In the country of Albania, a person was expelled from the church because she held a Bible study outside the church building. This Bible study was for Muslim seekers who wanted to learn more about Jesus. This should have been celebrated by the pastors, but it was viewed as a threat because it wasn't under their control.

Christ's approach was in stark contrast to the Pharisees and scribes. He came to a home as a special dinner guest, yet his feet were not washed, as was customary of honored guests. A sinful woman barged in with an expensive jar of ointment. She began pouring it on Jesus's feet and washing His feet with her tears and drying them with her hair. The host, a Pharisee named Simon, was appalled that Jesus would let a sinful woman even touch Him.

> And Jesus answered him, "Simon, I have something to say to you." And he replied, "Say it, Teacher." "A money-lender had two debtors: one owed five hundred denarii, and the other fifty. When they were unable to repay, he graciously forgave them both. So which of them will love him more?" Simon answered and said, "I suppose the one whom he forgave more." And He said to him, "You have judged correctly." (Luke 7:40–43)

Then we see grace lived out. We see the tenderness and gentleness of grace as Jesus dealt with Simon and the woman all at once. This is, perhaps, one of the best illustrations of grace in action in the New Testament.

> Turning toward the woman, He said to Simon, "Do you see this woman? I entered your house; you gave Me no water for My feet, but she has wet My feet with her tears and wiped them with her hair. You gave Me no kiss; but she, since the time I came in, has not ceased to kiss My feet. You did not anoint My head with oil, but she anointed My feet with perfume. For this reason I say to

you, her sins, which are many, have been forgiven, for she loved much; but he who is forgiven little, loves little."

Then He said to her, "Your sins have been forgiven." Those who were reclining at the table with Him began to say to themselves, "Who is this man who even forgives sins?"

And He said to the woman, "Your faith has saved you; go in peace." (Luke 7:44–49)

We are saved by His amazing grace. The Lord shows loving-kindness and mercy to us in infinite ways. We are recipients of abundant grace. Being recipients of grace means that as leaders we rise above our own self-interests. The needs of the Body and needs of individuals are of paramount importance. Like Jesus, let us show grace to those we influence. *Summary*: A leader who is being transformed by Jesus Christ is one… who is increasingly and personally gripped by the power and wonder of grace; has experienced brokenness and mercy; and who treats others with similar acceptance, mercy, and love.

*Reminder*: Assess yourself with the tool provided in Appendix A.

## Value Shift 3
## From "Power-Based Leadership" to "Servant Leadership"

When God opened the door to work in the former Soviet Union in the mid-1990s, many of us who went in noticed a sad phenomenon. Pastors and Christian leaders had taken on the persona of communist bosses. Their word ruled.

Then in the summer of 2001, when MentorLink first began public training, we went to Colombia, South America, to conduct training in the five largest cities. We talked about power leaders, described it briefly, and interacted with them about Jesus's teaching on servant leadership. One of them said, "Oh, what you mean is called a 'cauldio' leader!"—meaning a leader that acts like a Latino dictator. The culture of the world had become the culture of the church, and leaders lead in churches and ministries just like they did in the culture around it.

As we gained more experience, we realized that the way most ministry leaders operate in each part of the world is like power leaders of the culture—the Indian guru, Chinese mandarin, African chief, Arabic sheik, or Western CEO.

I know the temptation of power leadership. I know what it means to run over people, and I know the freedom of serving people and letting God build His church.

I identify with James and John who, through their mother, asked for power positions sitting one on His right and one on His left in Jesus's coming kingdom. Most leaders would also ask for the same. When the other ten heard about it, they raged in anger. The issue was not the request of sitting on the right or left in Jesus's kingdom, but that James and John dared to ask first. Behind their hot anger was ambition for the same power, influence, and perks that would come with being numbers one and two after Jesus. All twelve wanted to be great. They were each ambitious.

Jesus called all of them together and said, in effect, your ambition for influence and desire for greatness is not the issue but your strategy for attaining it in the kingdom is 180 degrees off. The issue, said Jesus, is not a position of power but rather taking a servant attitude and acting like one for the sake of others.

Jesus did not reprimand their ambition or desire for greatness. He made it clear such drives are welcomed in His kingdom, but the strategies, motives, values, and character needed to express these drives are of a different nature.

Moving from power, dominance, and position toward Jesus's expectations for leaders is not innate to the flesh. One has to learn to be a servant, to really look out for others' interests and put Jesus's kingdom first. Each of us desiring to lead in light of eternity will go through this journey of moving from the left to the right in our strategies, motives, and values.

Those who have large organizations or churches with many people and resources can easily be deceived into thinking that Jesus has authenticated their leadership. Numbers of people, size of organization, and position of power mean nothing to Christ. What the Lord mandated of leaders in His kingdom is that they be servants. This is radical, but in light of eternity, do I follow the ways of the flesh or the ways of Jesus?

In other places, I have written about my own struggles and identification with James, John, and the other ten disciples. Since my adoption into His family, I have been learning how to be a servant of Jesus and His saints. Some breakthroughs have occurred in my heart, and many failures have been apparent. My ambition and drives remain, and my strategies, heart, and values continue to shift toward Jesus's ways. May it be true of you as well. None of us has arrived.

*Summary*: A leader who is being transformed by Jesus Christ is one... whose influence and impact is not determined by position, power, or control but who influences and impacts others through serving them in the power of Christ.

*Reminder*: Assess yourself with the tool provided in Appendix A.

## Value Shift 4
## From "Elitism and Self-Sufficiency" to "Collaboration and Community"

I am a ministry pioneer or entrepreneur—doing new things or old things in new ways. This is my gifting and part of my calling. As a pioneer the temptation is to do something alone because no one else "sees it" or "understands it." Every time I've done something alone, it did not sustain over time.

I've learned several lessons that relate directly to this value shift. First, I've learned that you can go fast alone but you can go farther together. In other words, I can get something done by myself quickly, but if it is to be sustainable, it must be done as a group with others making contributions. I am not omnicompetent. I need insights, contributions, and gifts of others to compensate for my shortcomings, limited perspectives, and incomplete knowledge and wisdom.

Second, I've learned that it is easier to be pulled by a rope than to push something by a rope. Ropes only have one-way power when it comes to moving an object. Doing something by myself is like pushing something by a rope. There is a lot of movement, but not much is moved.

Things happen when others help and contribute through their spiritual gifts. We are collectively pulled by the rope of the Spirit.

God is known in relationship. Father, Son, and Holy Spirit collaborate to lead the universe and all creation. Each has specific roles, yet in perfect unity they hold things together. Though we have great difficulty understanding how the Trinity works, no one can miss that they collaborate. This is the perfect model of collaborative leadership. If the Trinity models this, should we not also do the same?

I enjoy watching basketball. Basketball reminds me that you can have a star player, but the team that usually wins is the one that plays the best team defense and offense. Basketball is a team sport. In the same way, leadership in His kingdom is designed to be a team effort, a collaboration of leaders each with different gifts, capacities, and responsibilities.

Observe the collaboration Paul reflects in sharing his heart with Timothy.

> Make every effort to come to me soon; for Demas, having loved this present world, has deserted me and gone to Thessalonica; Crescens has gone to Galatia, Titus to Dalmatia.

> Only Luke is with me. Pick up Mark and bring him with you, for he is useful to me for service. But Tychicus I have sent to Ephesus. When you come bring the cloak which I left at Troas with Carpus, and the books, especially the parchments. (2 Tim. 4:9—13)

> Greet Priscilla and Aquila, and the household of Onesiphorus. Erastus remained at Corinth, but Trophimus I left sick at Miletus. Make every effort to come before winter. Eubulus greets you, also Pudens and Linus and Claudia and all the brethren. (2 Tim. 4:19—21)

Note how many different names he listed. Paul was not a "lone-ranger" leader. Yet so many ministries are led by lone rangers. Jesus, Paul, and the disciples did not work this way. Leading in light of eternity means we will follow the model of the Trinity and of Jesus's apostles in working together with other leaders.

*Summary*: A leader who is being transformed by Jesus Christ is one… who resists the tendency to work alone and in isolation, either because of pride or unwillingness to share. This leader values relationships and is willing to use his or her strengths and work with others who are strong where he or she is weak.

*Reminder*: Assess yourself with the tool provided in Appendix A.

**Value Shift 5**
**From "Accidentally Adding Leaders" to "Intentionally Multiplying Leaders"**

MentorLink was envisioned at a small gathering of thirteen leaders from twelve ministries. We came from globally focused ministries, including Campus Crusade, Navigators, Wycliffe, Church Resources Ministries, World Team, United World Mission, and others. Collectively, we had shoe-leather leader-development experience in every continent of the world. Though none of us were experts, we were experienced.

We met for four days in November of 1999. Our goal was to answer the question, "How do we accelerate the development of Christlike leaders in the Body of Christ?" The chart below illustrates what we all observed as the increasing shortfall of Christlike leaders:

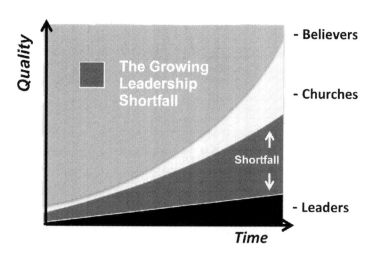

Many ministries focus on evangelism using the *JESUS* Film Project, crusades, media, personal evangelism, and many other forms. There are many denominations and ministries with evangelism as a primary focus. This is all good. Millions are coming to Christ.

Many ministries and churches focus on church planting. There are saturation church-planting strategies that work. Many churches are being planted around the world. This is all good.

We noticed that while the emphasis is on gaining new converts and new churches, there is little intentional emphasis on building new leaders to disciple new converts or shepherd new churches. This is what we call the "leadership shortfall." The shortfall is increasing exponentially.

The bottom line? Globally, the Body of Christ is in a leadership-shortfall crisis, and most are unaware.

Vast sums of money are spent on gaining new converts only to see "converts" disappear months later because there is no one to disciple and follow up. More money has to be raised again to reevangelize the area. Likewise, many man-hours are spent and much money was raised to plant new churches only to see many of these churches disappear months or several years later because there is no one to disciple and lead them.

Why is this happening? Because we are not following Jesus's model of intentionally developing leaders for our ministries.

Jesus came to offer salvation to the world. He had such a burden for the whole world, the billions that have been and will be born, that He intentionally focused on building the twelve. His vision was for the masses who come from every tongue, tribe, and nation. These are the billions who will be with Him in eternity. Because He had such a burden and because they all had to be reached, He focused on training and mentoring a couple of handfuls of leaders.

Jesus did not develop leaders by the now-popular model of "content transfer" in large groups. He did not seek to mass produce leaders in large numbers through exposing people to His brand of leadership. His model was simple. He intentionally picked a few and invested deeply in them.

Intentionally building leaders is His heart and strategy. Should we do anything different? We will look at this in some detail in chapter 6.

*Summary*: A leader who is being transformed by Jesus Christ is one…who chooses to make mentoring a priority in his or her life and ministry; he or she devotes time and effort toward raising up the next generation of leaders.

*Reminder*: Assess yourself with the tool provided in Appendix A.

## Overall Summary

Leading in the ways of the flesh is natural. It feels good, and it is practiced by many Christian leaders worldwide, but it is antithetical to the ways of Jesus. Jesus and His apostles reveal a different way. We are not left to our own to sort out how to lead in Jesus's kingdom.

## Prayer

*Lord, I want to abide in you and lead and walk as You did.* (1 John 2:6)

## Questions for Thought or Discussion

1. Look back over the five value shifts. Which one is easiest for you? Hardest?
2. Take some minutes to go through the personal assessments in Appendix A. Think through the questions at the end of each value-shift assessment.

# Chapter 4

## LEAD FROM INSIDE OUT

Recently, I met with a leader from another ministry who conducted training for pastors in Zambia using MentorLink's "Passing It On" materials. These pastors were wide-eyed with shock that the focus was on their own character, heart, values, and motives rather than ministry skills and knowledge. My friend shared how this emphasis impacted these leaders. No one had trained them like this before. It is amazing that something so simple and so right off the pages of the New Testament is missed by Bible colleges, seminaries, pastors, and teachers.

Another leader I know goes into remote areas of Ethiopia where he conducts similar training. Many leaders who are exposed to this training come to repentance and acknowledge they have been operating as false teachers. Often there are tears of confession with the repentance.

Almost twenty years ago, I was invited to attend a silent retreat. There were six of us in this beautiful mountain setting. Because it was a silent retreat, we could not talk with one another even at meals. The only person we could talk with was our spiritual director but only during our daily individual spiritual-direction time. This was a new experience for me. I had no idea what to expect.

During my first time with the spiritual director, he me gave an assignment to look at John 11 and view the situation from the perspective of Lazarus. I was tasked to answer the question, "What did Lazarus think, feel, see, hear, and smell as he was called back to life by Jesus's command?" Then he asked me to give names to the grave clothes that wrapped around me and had the stench of death. He said, "Give particular attention to the grave cloth that covered Lazarus's eyes and kept you from seeing Jesus."

At first I tackled the assignment as a Bible study. I spent a couple of hours studying it from Jesus's, Mary's, and Martha's perspectives and the overall situational context of Jesus's purposes in the Gospel of John. Then I began to personalize Lazarus's experience and naming the grave clothes in my own life.

I started typing on my old eight-pound (four-kilogram) Mac laptop. I began to slowly think through my life and sins. I spent the better part of a day on this and listed three pages of bullet points of sins going as far back as thoughts came to mind. Then I spent some time thinking and praying about what was keeping me from seeing Jesus. I discerned that my own fear of rejection was keeping me from seeing Jesus. I confessed these sins.

The apostle John came at this issue from another angle in his first letter.

> If we say we have no sin, we deceive ourselves, and the truth is not in us. If we confess our sins, he is faithful and just to forgive us our sins and to cleanse us from all unrighteousness. If we say we have not sinned, we make him a liar, and his word is not in us. (1 John 1:8–10)

What a comfort to think Jesus is the advocate for our sin (1 John 2:1).

I experienced Jesus's revolutionary grace and forgiveness at a heart level. With this list of sins in front of me, I sensed just how much Jesus forgave and loved me. Then I looked at John 12. What I learned was that Jesus is my friend and wants to be with me. Jesus loves me, likes me, and is my elder brother. Yes, He is my Lord, but I experienced His love and forgiveness at a deeper level.

Right after this silent retreat, I went to our CoMission training. The team of trainers who knew me well took one look at me and said, "What happened to you?" They could see from my countenance that I had a new peace or something. I shared how the Lord met me, had forgiven me, and how much He loves me.

Most of us serving the Good Shepherd want to bear fruit, see lives changed, and meet real needs. Jesus said, "By this my Father is glorified, that you bear much fruit and so prove to be my disciples" (John 15:8). But actions done in the flesh will not bring spiritual fruit. It is when we are in fellowship with Jesus and walking in the Spirit that spiritual results happen.

Jesus said, "I am the vine; you are the branches. Whoever abides in me and I in him, he it is that bears much fruit, for apart from me you can do nothing" (John 15:5). Note: Some English translations use "remain" instead of "abide."

If abiding or remaining in Jesus is so important, let's emphasize it in our own lives and ministries.

Here are some indicators of the abiding life:

1. We walk in the same way Jesus walked (1 John 2:6).
2. We love our brothers and sisters in Christ (1 John 2:10, 4:13, 4:16).

3. We hold to the Gospel we heard from the beginning (1 John 2:24).
4. We don't practice sin (1 John 3:6).
5. We practice righteousness (1 John 3:9–10, 3:24).
6. We are generous with our possessions (1 John 3:17–18).

The point is that abiding in Jesus is primarily an internal reality that works itself out in the way we live. This is inside-out transformation.

> *To lead in light of eternity is to lead from the inside out, staying in fellowship with Jesus; walking in His ways; and constantly checking our heart, character, motives, and values.*

Observe how Jesus rebuked leaders in Matthew 23. The Pharisees and scribes put emphasis on the outside or externals. It was hard to find fault with them based on the rules they set up, which were seen and measured on the outside. Jesus severely rebuked them for this. Their inside life was full of lawlessness, robbery, self-indulgence, and hypocrisy. He said to them, "First clean the inside of the cup."

Jesus values a heart abiding in Him, walking in the Spirit and clean on the inside. He is mindful of our weaknesses yet always makes intercession for us. I am convinced that people who read this book want to live for Jesus and lead in light of eternity. Otherwise, why would anyone read this far?

## What Is Leading from the Inside Out?

People evaluate us from the outside. That's all they can see. But God looks at the heart. To lead in light of eternity is to lead from the inside out, staying in fellowship with Jesus; walking in His ways; and constantly checking our heart, character, motives, and values.

Faithful servants from years past advocate spending time with Jesus each day. Many find it helpful to spend time with Him first thing each morning. This time dedicated to the Almighty has worship, prayer, reading or studying the Bible, and confession of known sins. The Word of God is sharper than any two-edged sword and is able to discern the thoughts and intentions of the heart (Heb. 4:12).

This book is about self-evaluation for leaders—evaluating ourselves from the outside and inside. Are we living in light of eternity? "Be holy in all your conduct," are the words of Peter (1 Pet. 1:17–18).

While I was working on one of the chapters in this book, I was thinking about the sin of envy, wondering how I might express that sin. What I saw in myself was not pretty. I confessed my sin. Confessing a sin is agreeing with the Father that He is right and then looking to Him for forgiveness through Christ. I can stand in His presence entirely by His grace through the finished work of the Lamb of God.

The issues are these: Are my character, heart, values, and motives aligning with Jesus? Am I living and walking in the Spirit? Am I abiding in Jesus? These are questions and issues any leader wanting to honor Jesus will be asking.

It is very helpful to have brothers or sisters who have the same heart and concern in your community. I need so much help that I have many different groups and mentors I relate to.

As I write this, I am at a coffee shop in Southern California, drinking coffee for another forty-five minutes before I see one of my mentors. One of the great challenges and motivators in my life has been to spend time with mentors over the years. These are men who are going before me in the walk of faith. Frankly, I am not sure where I would be if it was not for them and the wisdom and insight they offered me.

> *While I was working on one of the chapters in this book, I was thinking about the sin of envy, wondering how I might express that sin. What I saw in myself was not pretty. I confessed my sin.*

I have tried many things in my walk with Jesus to move toward the abiding life. I can say for certain, at least for me, there is no formula, no routine that guarantees a faithful walk. In the past I have been fed at various times by intense Scripture memory and meditation, by devotional reading and studying the Bible, or by deep study of a book in the Bible. For many years I was fed more from Paul's epistles and, more recently, from the Gospels. I've used devotional guides, Bible-reading guides, and other aides to my devotional life. They all had some value in my life and, of course, focused me on prayer and abiding in Jesus. Ultimately, it's not about the activities of spending time with Abba but about my relationship with Him. I find I am often in dialogue with the Great High Priest as I go through the day.

Outward disciplines, at least in my experience, do not guarantee an abiding life. But they are essential in providing a framework for right practice and living. Abiding is moment by moment and decision by decision. This is why it's called a struggle.

## Impediments to Christlikeness

One impediment to the abiding life is our understanding of Christian growth. There is a pervasive assumption in our Christian world that if we know the right answer, we are OK. The more we know, the more mature we are. For this reason we strive to learn more. We go to seminaries or Bible colleges thinking this will surely make us more spiritual. We begin our studies only to find out these environments are hazardous to a walk with Jesus. Please don't get me wrong, seminaries and Bible colleges are not the root cause; they only carry the assumption.

I am grateful for my seminary experience. We lived about forty-five minutes from the seminary. There were a number of students and a few professors living nearby, so we regularly carpooled. During the morning commute, we spent a good bit of the time praying for whatever came to mind and the pressing issues of our lives, families, churches, and ministries. On the return home, we talked about what we were learning.

My major was missions, but my informal major was hermeneutics (interpretation) because I had the privilege of carpooling with a professor who taught a number of classes on this subject. What a wonderful time of fellowship and growth these carpooling discussions were to me. What became apparent was that our classes assumed we had a walk with Jesus. We learned so much about the Bible, original languages, church history, preaching, Christian education, and theology. We were educated beyond our ability to apply and live out the Christian life.

No matter what we know, what our accomplishments or credentials are, our inside-out walk with Jesus is vital. Our relationship with Jesus is revealed by how we walk. Filling our heads with knowledge does not mean our walk with Jesus will be faithful.

Below are two graphics comparing the current emphasis of building Christians and leaders with the New Testament emphasis. These are not quantitatively precise, but they do illustrate the global emphasis from my observation and experience. Note: The "How-tos" refer to skills and programs.

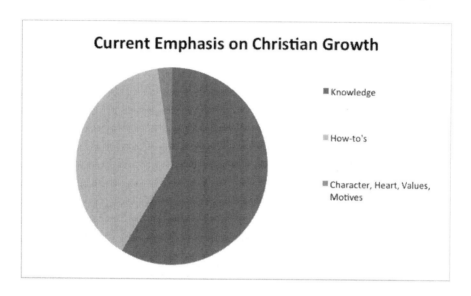

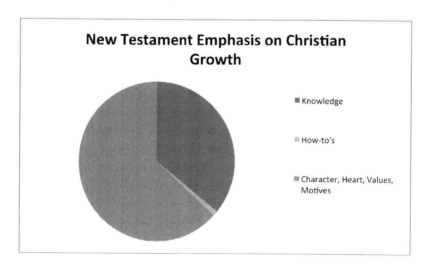

Fruits of the Spirit are love, joy, peace, patience, kindness, goodness, faithfulness, gentleness and self-control (Gal. 5:22–23). How many of these are knowledge based? They are inside-out expressions of abiding in Jesus. Just because we know what they are does not mean we are living them.

Knowing the right things and living them are two different things. Knowledge does have its place. Peter gives a summary of where knowledge fits. Most of these are inside-out character qualities.

> Make every effort to supplement your faith with virtue, and virtue with knowledge, and knowledge with self-control, and self-control with steadfastness and steadfastness with godliness, and godliness with brotherly affection, and brotherly affection with love. For if these qualities are yours and are increasing, they keep you from being ineffective or unfruitful in the knowledge of our Lord Jesus Christ. (2 Pet. 1:3–11)

> *"When the Pharisees noticed and began counting Jesus's disciples and baptisms compared to John the Baptist's, Jesus left and sought out one Samaritan woman. Jesus wanted nothing to do with metrics."*

Another impediment to our walk with God in our ministries is how we measure success. We brought the term "metrics" into our churches and ministries, adopted from the business world. These metrics measure externals. This has become a major issue in the Christian world. How do we measure spiritual results that are inside? If we only measure externals, we as financial contributors and ministry leaders push ourselves toward the patterns and practices of the Pharisees and scribes. Internal change is difficult and, at best, subjective to measure. Personally, I've found that ministry metrics undermine ministries and particularly ministries that emphasize inside-out transformation.

One of my mentors recently pointed out to me, "When the Pharisees noticed and began counting Jesus's disciples and baptisms compared to John the Baptist's, Jesus left and sought out one Samaritan woman (John 4:1–3). Jesus wanted nothing to do with metrics."

One of MentorLink's elders is Myron (Mike) Harrison. Mike served as field director for OMF (formerly China Inland Mission) in the Philippines. He spent his whole adult life as a missionary in that nation. Recently, he wrote an insightful short devotional at the end of one of MentorLink's Weekly Prayer Updates.

### The Lord Ponders Our Heart

We are much concerned with our outward appearance and demeanor before others. What will they think of me if I wear this outfit or perform in that way! The Lord, however, goes to the center of our being, our heart, and "ponders" or "weighs" the heart (Prov. 21:2, 24:12), and searches (Jer. 17:10) the heart in order to "know" (Luke 16:15) the true self and motives behind what we do and say!

To ponder (consider) or weigh (evaluate) the heart indicates that the Lord is most concerned about that which is on the inside and not necessarily concerned with the outside! We remember the call and anointing of David, the youngest son of Jesse, as king of Israel. When asked by the prophet Samuel if Jesse had any more sons, Jesse said, just one watching the sheep! Samuel then made that significant statement, "For the Lord sees not as man sees: man looks on the outward appearance, but the Lord looks on the heart" (1 Sam. 16:7).

Furthermore, the Lord searches (examines) our heart: "I the Lord search the heart and test the mind, to give every man according to his ways, according to the fruit of his deeds" (Jer. 17:10). Thus the Lord "knows" the heart of man (Luke 16:15) and is most capable of judging our actions, deeds, and motives.

What does our Lord observe and see when He "considers" our heart and why we do what we do? What will He find in your heart today? Is it honorable, respectable, or deceitful as we learned previously from Jeremiah?

Myron Harrison
Toronto, Canada


## Peer Mentors

Integrating what we know in our heads with how we live and lead is the real issue. Seeking answers and progress in most of these areas is much easier if we have mentors and peers.

One of my pastor friends from Senegal and Cameroon shared this:

Leading from the inside out is vital nowadays. In Senegal, at the beginning of each year, I choose one person (pastor, missionary, or a mature Christian) and ask him to tell me how he has seen both me and my ministry for the past year. By the end of our time together, I ask him to look me in the eyes and tell me three character things that he does not like in me. What he says, no matter how ugly it is, is what I focus on for the year, asking the Spirit of God to change me from the inside out.

I mentioned in passing a few pages ago that I am part of several groups of peers who serve in this capacity for me.

I met with two peer mentors every week for coffee and breakfast for over twenty-three years. We would talk about what was happening in our families, ministries, and lives and anything else that was on our minds. We all traveled, so if we met three times in a month, that was a lot. Sometimes only two of us were there. I always looked forward to our time.

I meet with two other groups once per year. When we gather, we are usually in a small house or hotel meeting room. We eat together, and over a period of two to three days, each takes about three to four hours to share whatever he wants. Then the brothers ask questions about any topic they want. These are transparent times together. Then we all pray for the brother who shared before we go to the next person. This is not sophisticated, but I personally feed off of the experience and their input for months.

My wife, Paula, has a variation of this for women. They call it "Summer Camp." These five women have been meeting for twelve years every June for five days at a remote cabin to talk and share their lives and hearts. They all have traveling ministries but schedule their whole spring and summer around the privilege of spending these days together. The way they do it is that each morning everyone is on her own for prolonged devotional times. Then they eat lunch together, take walks together, eat supper together, and talk well into the evening.

My wife and I are also in several couples' groups that meet periodically. These groups are for our own growth and community. We are not putting out but rather feeding our own souls with the love, care, challenge, and refining that happens when you are with like-minded people. Frankly, I don't know how Christian leaders who constantly minister to others make it without some version of what I experience. Ministry is too costly not to have others help us along the way.

You can do what Paula or I do with a group of peers you already know. Think through all the people you know. They don't have to be in your denomination, ministry organization, or line of work. It is probably better that they are not. Show them this chapter and ask if they would consider spending a couple of days together just sharing life and ministry. Do it just once to see how it works, and then if you all like the outcomes in your lives, do it another time. Do it one year at a time. The ideal numbers for this are four to six people. These people can be nearby or across the country. All you need is a low-cost place to meet away from your families and daily grind. Turn off your mobile phones, and choose to spend time with those who can help you lead from the inside out.

## Summary
In Moses's day there was a Tent of Meeting. Moses went to the tent daily to meet with the Lord. Joshua would accompany him, but when Moses left, it says, "Joshua would not depart from the tent" (Exod. 33:7–11). Every Israelite could go to the Tent of Meeting. Joshua was the only one mentioned who chose to spend time with God. We, like the Israelites, are as close to the Lord as we choose to be.

"When you said, seek my face, my heart said to You, Your face O Lord I will seek" (Ps. 27:8).

"But to this one I will look, to him who is humble and contrite of heart and who trembles at my word" (Isa. 66:2).

The questions are as follows: How close am I to Jesus? Am I abiding in Him right now? Am I trembling at His Word? Am I in fellowship with others?

**Prayer**

*Lord, with all my heart, I want to seek You.* (Col. 3:1–2)

**Questions for Thought or Discussion**
1. This chapter illustrates the emphasis on knowledge, skills, and character of today versus the New Testament. Draw a pie chart of what your ministry emphasis has been recently. What adjustments must you make?
2. Who is or can be your friend(s) to journey with in life and ministry? What steps can you take to begin or enhance the times together to encourage and build up one another?
3. What is the Holy Spirit saying to you from this chapter?

# Chapter 5

## The Leader's Covenant

We were well into our preparations for Cape Town 2010—the Lausanne Movement's Congress on World Evangelism held in October of 2010 in Cape Town, South Africa. The organizers expected four thousand leaders from two hundred nations to attend. I was a member of an ongoing Lausanne Committee called the Leader Development Working Group (LDWG). We were tasked to present a workshop at the Congress. Six months before the Congress, I was asked to come up with a summary of biblical leadership.

We didn't know what this summary would look like, but I was passionate and felt a stewardship before God to put all I had into this project. I served as the editor and facilitator of this effort that

*It became a succinct document (two sides of one sheet of paper), that summarizes Jesus's heart for spiritual leaders in His kingdom, who serve His people.*

involved over fifteen edits and interaction with LDWG committee members and others from around the globe. Overall there were thirty-five different people who at one time or another gave input. There were theologians, leader development specialists, pastors, missionaries, and national level leaders from various countries.

As it turned out, it became a succinct document (two sides of one sheet of paper), that summarizes Jesus's heart for spiritual leaders in His kingdom, who serve His people.

We handed the Leader's Covenant out at the end of our workshop with one thousand attending. It is now currently available on the www.MentorLink.org website.

Although I served as the editor, it is not something I could have written on my own. Frankly, in my opinion, it comes from the heart of Jesus as expressed through many servants who gave their time and talent to this project. To Him be the glory. Below is the full text of the covenant.

Think of these ten points as "aspirations" to be a Christlike leader. No one, certainly not me, has arrived. These "ten aspirations" point in the direction of heart, attitudes, dependence, and repentance needed to live, lead, and develop people like Jesus wants.

\*\*\*

**Introduction**

I praise God who called me to serve Jesus Christ as a leader among his people. With all my heart, I want to follow my Lord and leader, Jesus, in the way He lived, led, and developed people. I affirm that I want to grow in Christlikeness as a leader and help others in my sphere of influence do the same. By His grace I commit myself to be and lead more like Christ.

(Note: A "leader" in this covenant could be a pastor, apostle, elder, bishop, deacon, evangelist, teacher, missionary, parachurch worker, prophet, marketplace leader, small-group leader, educator, house-church leader, or anyone who wants to lead like Jesus. This includes men and women, young and old, vocational ministry workers and "laity.")

## 1. I am accountable to Jesus.

I am responsible to Christ my Lord. He will evaluate and reward me. I have been called to a life of service; joy; and sacrifice for my Lord, His kingdom, and His people. I admire leaders around the world who make significant sacrifices, even giving their lives for the sake of my Lord. I take comfort that God rewards those who serve and sacrifice for Him and His people. I grieve that some leaders act as though Jesus has nothing to say about their ministry, the way they treat people, or the way they lead. They also do things to be noticed publicly and in so doing, have their temporal reward. Yet I know that my Father, who sees in secret, honors and rewards those who do the right thing even if no one sees it. I humbly ask for courage, boldness, and faith to be pleasing to my Lord in the way I lead.
(Matt. 6:1–6, Matt. 16:24–27, Luke 18:28–30, John 5:22–23, 1 Cor. 3:10–15, 1 Cor. 4:5, 2 Cor. 4:11–18, 2 Cor. 5:9–10, 2 Cor. 10:12–18, 2 Tim. 4:18)

## 2. I will live like Jesus.

Christlike character is required for leadership and maintained by walking in Jesus's ways. I want to avoid being like the Pharisees of Jesus's day, who gave significant attention to external indicators of their leadership roles but whose hearts and character were far away from the Father. I acknowledge that in our day, sexual temptations are all around, yet our Lord calls us to live a life of purity and godliness in thought and action. I grieve that sometimes leaders do not act with integrity or speak truthfully with those they seek to serve. I am saddened that leaders sometimes act out of envy or jealousy toward other leaders or ministries and slander them or work to cause and maintain divisions. I desire to be more like Jesus from the inside out and to reflect his character in heart and life. (Matt. 23:23–28, John 15:1–5, Phil. 1:15–17, Phil. 3:17–19, 1 Thess. 2:1–12, 1 Tim. 3:1–13, Titus 2:11–15, 2 Peter 3:11–14, 1 John 2:6)

### 3. I will serve Jesus.

Jesus came preaching the kingdom of God—the rule and reign of God in the hearts and lives of his people. By contrast, human nature presses leaders toward building their own "kingdoms" or "empires." I am saddened that some leaders seek glory and accolades from people and in so doing replace a focus on Jesus with a focus on themselves. I affirm that my mission is to build Jesus's rule and reign in the hearts of His people. I also acknowledge that in serving Jesus, I am called to serve and nourish my family in a godly manner. I want to serve Jesus with all my heart. (Matt. 5:1–12, Acts 28:30–31, 2 Cor. 4:1–2, Phil. 2:9–13, 1 Tim. 3:1–5, 2 Peter 2:1–3, 3 John 9–11)

### 4. I will lead like Jesus.

When our Lord came to earth, He modeled and taught what He wanted leaders in His kingdom to be and do. He taught that we must operate in humility and meekness, take up our cross daily, and treat people with grace and gentleness. He did not force His authority on anyone. Jesus used His positional authority to guide, bless, and benefit those He led. He calls us to lead in the same way. Many leaders use their positional authority to "lord it over" people and instead use the world's way of power leadership practices and values. I am saddened that some leaders, even while speaking accurate doctrine, do not live as Christlike leaders. Their actions distort Christ's teaching on leadership, confusing those they are called to serve. I humbly ask for a heart to lead like Jesus. (Matt. 18:1–4, Matt. 23:1–12, Mark 10:42–45, 2 Cor. 11:12–21, 2 Tim. 3:1–13, Heb. 1:1–2, 1 Peter 5:1–5)

## 5. I will develop leaders.

One of Jesus's top priorities was to develop leaders. He did not mass-produce leaders but intentionally focused on a small number of them. I affirm that developing leaders as Jesus did calls me to build close, personal relationships with promising men and women, and to invest time in mentoring them. I affirm that the heart cry from many younger leaders around the world is for a spiritual mentor. I also acknowledge my calling to equip saints for ministry and to release them to serve as the Holy Spirit directs. I am aware that many leaders ignore this priority. I ask for grace and insight to intentionally equip saints and strengthen the hearts and lives of younger leaders.

(Matt. 4:18–22, Matt. 28:16–20, Luke 6:12–16, John 17:6–19, Acts 11:22–26, Acts 15:39–16:5, Eph. 4:11–16, Phil. 2:19–30, 2 Timothy)

## 6. I will seek His face.

Our Lord esteems and honors those who walk in humility and dependence on Him and who seek His face in fellowship and communion. Jesus gave us a pattern of regularly spending time alone with the Father to seek His heart and commune with Him in prayer. He did this even in the midst of many demands, pressures, and even harsh circumstances. Following Jesus's model, I want to seek Him regularly in personal communion and prayer. I know this will please Him and enable me to more align myself with Him, His ways, and His will. I also want to live within my human limits by taking regular times of rest (Sabbath) to restore my soul. I know this will mean withdrawing from the pressures of my world for periods of time. My heart is to serve Him in faithfulness all my days until He takes me home or returns in His glory. By His grace I want to seek his face.

(Isa. 66:1–2, Matt. 14:23, Matt. 26:36–39, Mark 1:35–39, Luke 4:42–43, Luke 5:16, Phil. 4:5–7, 1 Peter 5:6–8)

## 7. I will seek spiritual fruit.

I am chosen to bear fruit. Jesus taught and modeled that spiritual fruit comes from "abiding in Him." I acknowledge that I cannot manipulate spiritual results or spiritual changes in the lives of people by means of my human wisdom or self-generated pressures. My role is to faithfully give myself to people through my gifts and calling and leave the results to God. My heart is to follow Jesus in His ways, walk in the Spirit, and abide in Him so that He works through me to bear much fruit for His glory. (Matt. 7:15–20, Matt. 16:21–23, John 15:1–11, 1 Cor. 3:5–9, 2 Cor. 1:12, 1 Tim. 4:6–16, 1 John 2:3–6)

## 8. I will collaborate.

God the Father, God the Son, and God the Holy Spirit are One, with each Person fulfilling unique roles, yet acting in perfect harmony. Their collaborative leadership operates in the context of mutual submission yet each with appropriate authority for their roles and functions. I want to follow collaborative leadership modeled by the Trinity as the standard for leaders. I ask for grace to grow in serving and collaborating harmoniously with my fellow leaders.
(Matt. 28:16–20, John 5:22–23, John 16:13–15, John 17:21, Acts 13:1–3, Rm. 8:14–17)

## 9. I will faithfully steward money.

Jesus and the apostles regularly had others steward money entrusted to them. They taught and modeled stewardship and operated above reproach in the sight of God and people. I grieve that some leaders take financial advantage of people or fail to seek financial accountability of other godly leaders for funds given to the ministry. I acknowledge that the love of money corrupts and distorts a leader's ability to serve Jesus's kingdom and causes many leaders to fail the test of godliness. I also acknowledge that leaders need to support their families and can rightly expect support from those they serve. I humbly ask for grace to walk above reproach before God and people with the finances entrusted to me.

(Matt. 6:25–34, Luke 16:14–15, Acts 4:32–5:11, Acts 6:1–7, Acts 20:25–35, 1 Cor. 9:1–18, 2 Cor. 8:16–22, 1 Tim. 6:9–11, 1 Peter 5:2–3, Jude 11–12)

## 10. I will use wineskins to serve.

Systems and organization ("wineskins") are aspects of stewardship for churches and ministries. I am stunned that in Jesus's day the Pharisees and scribes opposed Jesus by using their wineskins of traditions, organization, laws, credentials, and theology against Him. I am saddened that many leaders are similarly tempted and often succumb to drawing people's allegiance to themselves and their organization, methods, materials, or theological systems rather than to Christ. I observe that sometimes leaders want to be the ones in charge, so they create hierarchies, positions, and titles to enforce their control and dominance. It is easy to "lord it over" or abuse people by imposing plans, vision, or organizational mandates on people. I long to purify myself and to serve my King in holiness and gentleness and draw those I serve into a closer walk with Him.

(Matt. 23:13–33, John 11:47–48, 53, Acts 20:18–35, Phil. 2:19–21, James 4:13–16, 1 Pet. 5:2–3, 3 John 9–11)

## Conclusion

I am standing on the shoulders of leaders who have gone before me. They were not perfect, and neither am I. They led based on what they had been taught, and the Lord, by his grace and kindness, advanced His kingdom through them.

I confess my own failings as a leader before my Lord Jesus.

I humbly commit myself in the name of the Father, Son, and Holy Spirit to be more like Jesus and develop others who will also do the same. May God, by His grace and mercy, help me to be faithful to this covenant. Amen.

Joining with leaders around the world, I make this my personal covenant.

Signed_____

Date_____

Witness_____

Witness_____

You may find it helpful to spend devotional time going through the Scriptural references.

We encourage you to distribute this to others. Electronic copies for distribution can be obtained at www.MentorLink.org. Permission granted to distribute this Leader's Covenant without modification. ©MentorLink 2010.

The Leader's Covenant is built on the foundation of the Lausanne Covenant, 1974. This Leader's Covenant was developed for the Lausanne Leadership Development Working Group as a resource for Cape Town 2010 Congress on World Evangelization.

Editor's note: Please e-mail editorial comments to info@MentorLink.org.

\*\*\*

There are many ways the covenant can be used in our own lives, work, and ministries. One of my colleagues uses it as a basis for mentoring leaders. He meets individually with a number of men. The first ten times they meet, the covenant is part of the discussion.

It could be used for elders, boards, teachers, or groups of leaders who gather to share what God is doing in their lives.

I frequently use it as a devotional guide as a checkup on my heart and practices of leading. I never leave it without confessing some sin and feeling deeply challenged to be more like Jesus.

> *I frequently use it as a devotional guide as a checkup on my heart and practices of leading. I never leave it without confessing some sin and feeling deeply challenged to be more like Jesus.*

Recently, I was in Dakar, Senegal, attending a West Africa conference. At a coffee break, I struck up a conversation with a senior African leader. He asked me what our ministry was about. I shared about some of our training and mentoring ministry. Then he asked about resource materials we used. I described a few pieces and had a copy of the Leader's Covenant with me and pulled it out to show him. He saw it and got big eyes. He said, "We use this with all our new African staff and ask them to sign it before they are accepted in our mission."

How does the Lord want you to use it?

**Prayer**

*Lord, give me eyes to see, ears to hear, grace to walk, and spiritual power to live and lead according to the Leader's Covenant.*

**Questions for Thought or Discussion**

1. What has the Lord impressed on you after reading the Leader's Covenant?
2. How can you use it in ministry?
3. Who else should know about the covenant in your ministry or network of friends?

# Chapter 6

## DEVELOP LEADERS LIKE JESUS

There were two leaders named Sam and Tim, both deeply burdened about the need to develop leaders. They were good friends and talked many times about their common burden. Then Sam and Tim both decided that talk was just talk and that they needed to get off the fence and do something. They started taking action steps in the same year.

Sam had a strategy that was high impact and would produce large, immediate growth in new leaders. He determined to host a leadership conference for three days and recruit one thousand people to his event. He would be the featured speaker and use his motivational gifts to teach and excite the crowd to be leaders. His topics included vision; strategy; leadership skills; management skills; cutting-edge thinking on organizations; recruiting skills; and, of course, some Bible here and there to make sure it was spiritual. He did this for ten years, each year producing one thousand new leaders. At the end of ten years, he had trained ten thousand leaders. "Remarkable" is what almost anyone would say.

Tim said to himself, "I don't want to use Sam's strategy. It's too time consuming for the results. I want to build a sustainable leader-development movement. I don't know one thousand people and don't have the gifts to pull off a three-day conference. I don't think the conference approach really works, anyway!" So Tim did what he knew to do: he recruited and mentored two leaders each year who also recruited and mentored two leaders each year, who also recruited and mentored two leaders each year. This went on year after year, multiplying mentors and mentees. The mentoring consisted of prayer, Bible study, and looking at the ways of Jesus and Paul and the New Testament church. It also consisted of letting the mentees see the issues and struggles of the mentor and talk and pray over the issues the mentee faced. This went on for ten years.

Then right after they finished their tenth year, they both went to a conference about leadership development in another country. Sam would be one of the featured speakers because of his massive work in this area. Tim went because he was Sam's friend and wanted to learn more about developing leaders. They got on the plane together, but shortly after takeoff, their plane developed catastrophic engine problems and crashed during the attempted emergency landing. All on board were killed. Sam's death was headlined in many papers and blogs.

**Revealing Questions**

1. At the end of ten years, which strategy produced more leaders? Sam's or Tim's?
2. What happened to Sam's leadership-development strategy in year eleven?
3. What happened to Tim's leadership-development strategy in year eleven? Year twelve? Year thirteen and on?
4. Which strategy got the attention?
5. Which leader got the glory?
6. Which leader got significant funding?
7. Which leader followed the way of Jesus?
8. Which leader do you want to be like?

**Jesus's Burden**

What would you be thinking about if you had less than twenty-four hours left to live? I've not been in that situation, so I can only imagine. I believe most of us would only be thinking about what was most important and our most important relationships. We have a glimpse into Jesus's priorities and important relationships less than twenty-four hours before He died. Also by looking into His last recorded lengthy conversation with the Father, in John 17, we understand Jesus's macro strategy.

This is simply put, below:

- Jesus came to glorify the Father, and He asked that the Father glorify Him (John 17:1–5).
- Jesus came to develop leaders (v. 6–19), and He kept all but Judas (v. 12). He mentions the twelve thirty-one times (them, they, those, themselves). The twelve were the most important people to Jesus. It was through the twelve minus Judas that He would reach and lead the masses.
- Jesus's third priority was the masses—those who would believe in Him through their word (v. 20–26).

This simple overview of John 17 is most instructive to us in this discussion because Jesus reveals His strategy and intentionality in building leaders for the masses. Jesus mentions the twelve thirty-one times, encased in thirteen verses. His priority and strategy for developing leaders is clear to all who have eyes to see in the four Gospels. If not, His last discussion with the Father reveals His set of priorities. Note: For a complete discussion on this see A. B. Bruce's classic book, *The Training of the Twelve* (Kregel Publications, 1971, p. 449–462).

Jesus had such a burden for the whole world, the masses of people of all generations, that He chose to intentionally invest in the twelve. He could have used Sam's strategy. After all, He could captivate the masses,

He was popular, and people went to great personal effort to see and hear Him. But He did not do this. Instead, He chose twelve to be with Him. He set up a sustainable and exponentially growing leader-development strategy.

> *Jesus had such a burden for the whole world, the masses of people of all generations, that He chose to intentionally invest in the twelve.*

We see Jesus's priority on the twelve, but we choose to ignore it to our own hurt. Leaders continue to be enamored with big-name leaders who collect large crowds so they can pass on their leadership gems. We think there is sustainability and power in the mass model, but there is not.

Another way we practically ignore Jesus's priority of building leaders is that we put our efforts into building and leading organizations instead. Some of the best people, who can and should focus on developing leaders, are instead focused on building ministry organizations or running church programs.

## Look Around

There is a global, pervasive burden of younger men and women who want an older person to mentor them. They know the power of a mentor because they've been told mentors are important. Mentors are key to personal growth in a career and in life in general. These young people probably did not have a good relationship with their father, so in some ways they want a father, minus the lectures. Yet my generation of leaders places little priority on mentoring. We miss so much by neglecting younger people and rejecting Jesus's priority and strategy of mentoring the next generation of leaders.

In preparation for the Lausanne Congress on World Evangelism, Cape Town, 2010, the Leadership Development Working Group conducted a survey with over one thousand younger leaders from around the world. When they were asked the question "If you had the opportunity to take classes in leadership development right now, what subjects would be of most interest to you?" They chose these from the list provided in this order:

- Mentoring and coaching (by a vast majority)
- Prayer and the personal life of a leader
- People management
- Conflict resolution
- Strategic planning

Even administrators at a secular high school understand the importance of mentors. Recently, a Pinehurst, North Carolina, high school distributed a sheet for its seniors to sign up as mentees to receive mentoring with someone in the community. Over two hundred students signed up. There was a call from the high school that went to churches and civic clubs for mentors to sign up. Only eight showed up. One of my longtime friends was among the eight.

Men and women, it is time to arise and shine. Younger generations need you and, more importantly, want you to lend your heart, time, and wisdom to their growth.

### Jesus's Call

Some of Jesus's last words to His followers were in the form of a command. He said, "As you go, *make disciples* of the peoples, teaching them to obey all I have commanded you…" (Matt. 28:19–20). He said this in the context of His position as Lord, "All authority has been given me in heaven and on earth" (Matt 28:16). So when the King, the Lord, and the One to whom every knee on earth will bow says something, it is priority. These are not optional words, nor are they to be treated as simple wishes for His undershepherds. These are words of action and words by which we will be held accountable when we stand before the Lord of Lords and King of Kings.

To put it another way, making disciples is a big deal to Jesus. He did not say, give them content or make them feel good, but rather teach them to obey all I've commanded. The discipling process is not left to our invention either. Rather, He shows us how to do it in principle. He was with them, patiently interacting with them in their struggle to believe and apply the truths He taught. He did not say, make them attend a church. A church attendee is not necessarily a disciple.

He said, "Make disciples." A disciple is one who obeys Jesus and follows Him. Disciples of Jesus are those who delve into the Word and obey what He says. Their heart, values, motives, and character come more aligned with Jesus and His kingdom ways as they grow in Christ.

Many of us think we are doing right things in our ministries because we compare ourselves and our ministries with those around us. However, the question is "What does Jesus want?" There is a different calling for each of us. Our part in making disciples will look different from person to person and culture to culture. If He is Lord, and He is, then what He wants and how He measures ministry is what counts. The Lord Himself will evaluate us with how we did in making disciples.

## Jesus's Power Model

Jesus used twelve powerful principles to train and develop kingdom workers. These practical principles are relevant for each leader seeking to lead in light of eternity.

1. The power of prayer
2. The power of intentionality

3. The power of small
4. The power of selection
5. The power of multiplication
6. The power of together
7. The power of equipping
8. The power of promise
9. The power of powerlessness
10. The power of blessing
11. The power of commissioning
12. The power of the Holy Spirit

## 1. The Power of Prayer

Jesus was a man of action and prayer. No one can miss His emphasis on prayer. Before He even began His public ministry, He spent forty days in the wilderness praying.

Prayer was part of His daily life and fellowship with the Father. His disciples were so curious that they requested, "Teach us to pray." His prayers were simple. He asserted that one should not make a show of praying. He practiced it daily and at all times. He spent the whole night in prayer reviewing His selection of the twelve. The twelve were prayed for throughout their time with Jesus. We know of Jesus's recorded prayer in John 17 where He refers to them thirty-one times in verses 6 through 19.

In John 17:6–19, Jesus prayed the following:

- For their faithfulness to God's Word (6)
- For them to see the reality of Who Jesus is (7–8)
- For them personally and collectively (9)
- That Jesus be glorified in them (10)
- For them to be kept in the Father's name (11a)
- For their oneness of heart and mind (11b)

- That they be guarded in the Father's name (12)
- That they have Jesus's joy fulfilled in them (13)
- That He had given them the Father's word and therefore was hated by the world (14)
- That they be kept from the evil one (15)
- That they are not of the world (16)
- That they would be set apart in the truth of the Word (17)
- That they would be sent into the world even as I was sent (18)
- That they would be set apart in the truth (19)

Prayer is vital to our collective growth, fruitfulness, protection, and developing leaders. One thing I do beyond praying for those I mentor is to bring them to our prayer network. There are faithful people who regularly pray for me and those I minister to and with. The MentorLink movement sends out a weekly prayer update to many who pray for specific people in the network. I write up the prayer needs weekly, usually on Friday morning, and send it to a faithful volunteer who prepares it to send to our prayer network on Sunday evening. We have a picture with that person's prayer needs. We ask people to pray for two people per day, so we cover fourteen in one week. Preparing the weekly prayer update for the following week is the most important hour I invest in the week.

We know this is significant in building people in their faithfulness to Jesus and His ways. It is also important protection from harm. Some in our network live and minister in difficult places in the world where their lives are on the line every day. Their families are threatened, and just getting from one place to another is exhausting and dangerous.

## 2. The Power of Intentionality
When Jesus began His public ministry, He knew the end from the beginning. He knew His season of public ministry would be short. He knew when and how He would be sacrificed for the sins of the whole

world. He was not hurried but moved and operated with purpose. He was intentional about developing disciples and leaders. Many followed Him, and He turned none away who sought the kingdom.

He knew leaders could not be mass produced but could be developed with intentional effort. So He chose twelve from among His many disciples to be leaders and began intentionally training and equipping them. They began the internal process of becoming kingdom leaders. Among the twelve He also gave special attention to the three—Peter, James, and John. This was not by accident.

Jesus planned to develop leaders for the kingdom with singular purpose. Proverbs says, "The plans of the diligent lead surely to advantage but everyone who is hasty comes surely to poverty" (Prov. 21:5). We understand His plan by what He did.

I have tried many approaches to develop leaders throughout my ministry years. I always had a plan, but it never worked out in the exact way I planned. Regardless, I move and operate intentionally to develop leaders. Jesus was intentional about everything He did. May He give you wisdom to apply this principle in your life and ministry.

## 3. The Power of Small

Small, little, and least are words used to describe the way of God in the Bible. He took one man from Haran and gave him a promise that through him all nations of the earth would be blessed and his descendants would be as numerous as the stars of the sky and the sand of the seashore. Gideon won a great battle with only three hundred men. God took David, the least of his brothers, and made him king. He took David and through him slew Goliath. The Lord is not impressed by the strength, intellect, credentials, or power of a man, but He does work through the humble, contrite, weak, and lowly. Jesus taught about the mustard seed.

Jesus did not take the elite of the nation to be His followers nor existing leaders from the religious system. He took common laborers, small-business owners, a political activist, a national traitor collecting taxes for the oppressors, a doubter, and a thief. These were men from the villages rather than the big city. They were not educated with significant degrees nor did any have wealth with the exception of perhaps Matthew because of his former tax-collecting career. He took the small, the least, and the little of this world and built a great following because of this powerful principle. He used the power of small to start with the twelve and through them built the church.

## 4. The Power of Selection

Think of the big heads each of the twelve must have developed when they were personally chosen by name out of hundreds of disciples. No wonder they kept arguing among themselves which of them was the greatest. Jesus had chosen them! This was a mark of honor and privilege. They saw things no one else did. They were insiders with the best-known prophet, teacher, and healer of their day.

Before He chose them, they had chosen Him. They were part of the crowds seeking to hear, see, and get closer to Jesus. He must have seen something in each one of them that He knew to be real. He saw their potential and their willingness to sacrifice if only a little.

I marvel that Jesus picked Matthew. Tax collectors of the day had a skill to quickly assess a person's ability to be taxed. They thought in financial terms. Matthew records many of Jesus's references to money. Many tax collectors were also adept at a form of shorthand. Matthew's Gospel has lengthy transcripts of Jesus's teachings, all because of his ability to record Jesus's words. Jesus saw this talent and knew it would be put to good use.

Jesus knows the heart of man. He knows that those who are chosen are more motivated to excel at what they are chosen for. This is a drive that played into the principles He used to build leaders.

## 5. The Power of Multiplication

MentorLink partnered with the *JESUS* Film Project to repurpose the film for discipleship and distribute it for follow-up, discipling, and leader development. We call this **40 Days with Jesus.** In May of 2012, I was in Arusha, Tanzania, delivering our first Days with Jesus in the Swahili language to be distributed initially through our partner, Here's Life Africa.

While in Arusha, I spoke one Sunday morning at the main Anglican church. I wanted to show the power of multiplication. I pulled out of my wallet two different bills in US dollars. I had a one-dollar bill and a one-hundred-dollar bill and showed the congregation. When they saw the one-hundred-dollar bill, their eyes got quite large. One hundred dollars represented a monthly income for many in Arusha. What I said to them follows:

> I want to illustrate multiplication to you with these two bills. I will give you a choice, though I will not give the money. You have two options:
>
> 1. You can have one hundred dollars each day for thirty days. This is three thousand dollars (equal to two and a half years of pay).
>
> 2. Or you can have one dollar doubled each day for a month. This means one dollar today, two dollars tomorrow, four dollars the next day, eight dollars the following day—for thirty days.

> You must choose right now. How many want one hundred dollars each day for a month? Raise your hands.

Surprisingly, well over half raised their hands. Then I shared the amount that would be given at the end of the month for those who had chosen $1 doubled each day—it was over $536,870,000. This is staggering—this is the power of multiplication.

Many of us understand the issue clearly when it comes to money. It is the same when it comes to developing leaders. No need to attempt to mass produce leaders. It won't work; it's too costly, and it is shortsighted, just like the people who chose one hundred dollars each day. Jesus used the other strategy, the powerful principle of multiplication.

Paul advocates a four-generation multiplication mind-set for leaders: "The things you have heard from me in the presence of many witnesses, these entrust to faithful men who will be able to teach others also" (2 Tim. 2:2).

## 6. The Power of Together

Jesus selected the twelve to be with Him and to see His life and ministry up close. Together they experienced His trials, miracles, accolades, and rejection. They were sent out two by two to go to the villages. They felt their own failures, successes, and questions. They heard His teachings and saw responses from all kinds of people. Life imparted life. He looked forward to the Last Supper. They celebrated it together.

When Jesus was about to be betrayed in the garden, He asked Peter, James, and John to join Him nearby while He prayed. He wanted them with Him. After His resurrection He met the disciples at various times and in different-sized groups but always together. Then He told them to wait in Jerusalem together "until the Holy Spirit has come upon you" (Acts 1).

John never got over being together with Jesus. Notice all the references to "we," "our," and "us" when decades later, the apostle John wrote the following:

> What was from the beginning, what we have heard, what we have seen with our eyes, what we have looked at and touched with our hands, concerning the Word of Life—and the life was manifested and we have seen and testify and proclaim to you the eternal life, which was with the Father and was manifested to us—what we have seen and heard we proclaim to you also, so that you too may have fellowship with us; and indeed our fellowship with the Father, and with His Son Jesus Christ. (1 John 1:1–3)

Paul was always with others. He trained Timothy, Titus, Silas, and others in the context of "together." The Jesus way of life, leadership, and ministry is "together."

## 7. The Power of Equipping

The twelve were with Jesus. They saw how He did ministry and how He treated people. His tenderness, gentleness, and compassion for the poor and oppressed were evident. They saw His heart for the lost sheep and the masses without shepherds. He rebuked hypocrites and false leaders. They were with Him when He healed, raised the dead, and cast out demons. They learned sacrifice, suffering, obedience, and servanthood. They went through faith tests of being in a storm on the sea about to drown and then saw Jesus still the storm.

He fed the five thousand and the four thousand, and His disciples where right there picking up leftovers, and each had a basketful to himself for his own meal. He sent them out two by two to the villages of the lost sheep of Israel to preach the good news of the kingdom, heal the sick, and cast out demons.

When Christ triumphantly entered Jerusalem on a donkey colt, His disciples were with Him. They saw Him crucified.

Through all this his disciples heard Him explain Himself. They must have had personal conversations with Him about many things. Jesus was not like an Indian guru, high and lofted up, remote and removed from interaction. Though He was God incarnate, He was also a man just like us. Yet He was so different in His character, heart, values, motives, and teaching that He had to be observed up close and personal for the twelve to understand.

Jesus didn't focus on how-tos (programs, methods, or skills) but rather on heart, character, values, motives, faith, and leading in light of eternity among other things. We would do well to emphasize the same in our equipping. Then He commissioned them. There was an end to His training.

During the years when former Soviet Union opened up, I was part of the CoMission—a movement of mostly lay people sent to serve at least one year as missionaries. I was amazed to see how the just-in-time training we gave people was put to use. If we train people and release them to minister, God will use them.

**8. The Power of Promise**
Throughout Jesus's ministry, He gave promises to the twelve. Here are some. What others come to mind?

- "Come to Me all you who are weary and heavy laden and I will give you rest."
- "I am the resurrection and the life; he who believes in Me will live even if he dies, and everyone who lives and believes in Me will never die."
- "Every branch that abides in Me bears much fruit."
- "Ask in My name and it will be given you."

What we must remember is that the power is in the Gospel, and God has graciously chosen to use His people. His promises are sure.

It is fitting that Jesus, the Lord and Savior, told the twelve, "All authority has been given me in heaven and on earth." Then He commissioned them to "make disciples." Some of His final words are words of promise: "Lo, I am with you, even to the end of the age" (Matt. 28:20). Our role is to point people toward Jesus's promises.

### 9. The Power of Powerlessness

It seems strange to our flesh to even mention this principle. We strive to be powerful, to have symbols of power, trophies of our conquests, results of our efforts, and stories boasting of our exploits. The twelve were obsessed with who was the greatest (read, "most powerful"). Power is what we crave in the flesh.

Jesus lived the opposite way. He emptied Himself and became obedient to the Father's will and direction. He only did what He saw the Father doing. He was obedient, submissive and dependent. This is powerlessness. It is the opposite of self-sufficient, arrogant, and operating in human wisdom.

He taught His disciples to do the same. What power does a servant have? None. Servants were the lowest people. He taught them that kingdom leaders were required to be servants and to empty themselves in obedience to the King.

He taught that sacrifice and obedience to the King and His kingdom principles would be rewarded. Peter said to Him,

> Behold, we have left everything and followed You. Jesus said, "Truly I say to you, there is no one who has left house or brothers or sisters or mother or father or children or farms, for My sake and for the gospel's sake, but that he will receive a hundred times as much now in the present age, houses and brothers and sisters and mothers and children and farms, along with persecutions; and in the age to come, eternal life. But many who are first will be last, and the last, first." (Mark 10:28–31)

*Leaders who understand this lead differently from leaders who lead by power. In developing leaders, our goal is to help people see this principle and, more importantly, grow in powerlessness.*

He told them that He would demonstrate the power of powerlessness by being the ultimate servant and dying on the cross. "For the Son of man did not come to be served but to serve and give His life as a ransom for many" (Mark 10:45).

Jesus suffered the most humiliating and painful execution. He used no power though He could have called on legions of angels. He took the way of powerlessness. When Jesus died, He truly died humbled, mocked, and abused as a common criminal. Yet through His powerlessness, He defeated Satan and death. He triumphed through His death on the cross and now reigns forever and ever as King of Kings and Lord of Lords.

Paul says it this way:

> [Jesus] emptied Himself, taking the form of a bondservant, and being made in the likeness of men. Being found in appearance as a man, He humbled Himself by becoming obedient to the point of death, even death on a cross. For this reason also, God highly exalted Him, and bestowed on Him the name which is above every name. (Phil. 2:7–9)

> Therefore I am well content with weaknesses, with insults, with distresses, with persecutions, with difficulties, for Christ's sake; for when I am weak, then I am strong. (2 Cor. 12:10)

Leaders who understand this lead differently from leaders who lead by power. In developing leaders, our goal is to help people see this principle and, more importantly, grow in powerlessness.

## 10. The Power of Blessing

In our day we underestimate the power of blessing people, particularly our children and those we seek to build in the faith. Abraham was blessed by God. He blessed Isaac. Isaac blessed Jacob through Jacob's deception. Esau sold his birthright and blessing for a bowl of lentil stew.

Jesus blessed the twelve at the Last Supper. He did it in a way that shocked them—He washed their feet. He was the Lord of the universe, creator of all, and King of Kings. He knew who He was and where He was going—to be seated at the right hand of the Father. With all of this knowledge, He laid aside His robes and girded a towel about Himself, took the role of the lowliest servant in the household, and washed their feet. One by one, tenderly and in a way that blessed and humbled each one.

When He finished, He told them what He did: "Do you know what I have done to you?" (John 13:12). He said in effect, "I am Lord and teacher, but I washed your feet. I took the low road and lifted you up. I blessed you and so you should do the same." He called them friends (John 15:14–15). "If you know these things, you are blessed if you do them" (John. 13:17).

I recently returned from Alexandria, Egypt, where I began a yearlong mentoring process with a group of six younger leaders (age twenty-nine to forty) from Egypt. These men all have broad ministries with a variety of organizations and churches. We met face to face for three days and now continue with monthly mentor group meetings via Skype. In addition I talk periodically with each one on personal issues. At the end of the three days, I read John 13 and then took a towel and using a bucket from the kitchen, I washed their feet. I blessed them in a way that they will not soon forget. Not with words but with actions. They felt what the twelve felt, and I felt the humiliation of Jesus at taking their feet and rinsing and washing each foot with water then drying each foot with a towel. Though I am the mentor, following Jesus's pattern, I blessed them by elevating them.

Wherever we go in the MentorLink network, we wash people's feet as a way of symbolizing our servant attitude and blessing people. Outside of Beijing, China, we conducted training for a group of house-church leaders. We asked the leader if we could do this. He was reluctant at first and said it wasn't done in China. We replied that this is what Jesus did, and we would like to do it. He said "OK, but only with volunteers." He volunteered first, and then one by one each person volunteered. There were spontaneous worship songs. Many people were weeping. It was such an exhilarating worship experience. We were all blessed.

Paul blessed Timothy in a different way. We see in 2 Timothy his reminders and exhortations. We see his tenderness toward his son in the faith. Like a father, he blessed him with this letter. Still in all the New Testament, 2 Timothy is my favorite letter. I find myself coming back to it again and again. In a way, each time I read it, I receive Paul's blessing. May you find the words and actions to bless those you develop and mentor.

## 11. The Power of Commissioning

Jesus commissioned the disciples for a purpose. He said, "As you go, make disciples…" (Matt 28:19–20). We know this as the Great Commission. There is an end point in our development. We don't develop people just to develop them—there is a purpose, a vision, something bigger than them. We marry; have children; and raise them to be functioning adults who will also marry, have children, and so on. We were born to reproduce. In the same way Jesus commissions us to nurture spiritual children who will also grow and reproduce and nurture other spiritual children.

When we commission a person, we say, "I believe in you," "I affirm your direction," and "I am behind you." These are words of hope, empowerment, and purpose. The power of commissioning cannot be overestimated. Jesus does this with each of us in the Great Commission, but there is also a need for human words.

Paul's second letter to Timothy is evidence of this. Take a minute to scan this short letter and note how many reminders and ways Paul commissions Timothy for future ministry. There is so much love, hope, and vision imbedded in these four chapters. Paul developed Timothy over a long period of time, but now his time was near—he had fought the good fight and kept the faith. He reminded Timothy that "In the future there is laid up for me the crown of righteousness, which The Lord, the righteous Judge, will award to me on that day..." (2 Tim. 4:7–8).

## 12. The Power of the Holy Spirit

Jesus was led by the Spirit into the wilderness to be tempted by the devil for forty days. When He was baptized, the Holy Spirit descended on Him like a dove. During His last meal with the twelve, He taught specifically and in detail the role of the Holy Spirit (John 14–16). The Spirit was a constant part of Jesus's experience and fellowship. The twelve observed this. He taught the twelve that the Spirit would be with them, counsel them, teach them, remind them, and lead them after He left.

He told His disciples to wait in Jerusalem for the promised Holy Spirit who would empower them to be His witnesses even to the remotest part of the earth (Acts 1).

The apostles further explained the Spirit's role. Inner change and repentance comes by the work of the Spirit. Doing kingdom work is accomplished through the work of the Spirit.

Ministry activities, programs, and organization can be done in the power of the flesh, but spiritual results cannot be accomplished without the power and work of the Holy Spirit. Developing people to understand this principle is vital to us.

## Jesus's Principles

Jesus used these principles to build leaders for His kingdom. We can use them as well. These are not methods but rather kingdom principles. They are supracultural—that is, they can be applied to any culture. How they are applied in Africa might be different from in India, Latin America, or Central Asia. These are not programs, curriculums, or methodologies but rather guidelines to focus and shape building new leaders for the kingdom.

*When we build people, we build them with a focus on Jesus and His kingdom. We are not making disciples of ourselves, our church, or our organization but rather of Jesus. This distinction is subtle but important.*

These are the questions to ask: Can we see these powerful principles at work in our ministries? Are we applying Jesus's power in developing others?

It is also important to note that when we build people, we build them with a focus on Jesus and His kingdom. We are not making disciples of ourselves, our church, or our organization but rather of Jesus. This distinction is subtle but important.

Every leader and ministry can apply Jesus's principles. Multiplying leaders for the kingdom also multiplies the ministry and the life of a leader. Children-at-risk workers, evangelists, church planters, pastors, economic-development workers, and any leader seeking to do kingdom work can follow these principles. They can be applied in the workplace, home, school, neighborhood, church, or ministry.

## How?

Jesus did not give us a program to follow, nor did He provide a curriculum or body of content to master. Learning styles, cultural realities, communication practices, and available technologies all vary from place to place and generation to generation. However, He did give principles we can apply in many ways.

Experienced leader developers will have their own preferences for how to develop leaders. Each leader has his or her own cultural context, available resources and technologies, learning styles, ministry platform, spiritual gifts, capacities, and mentees. Some are more effective than others. The issue really isn't knowing how to do it but rather wanting to do it.

If you are ready to get started, I suggest downloading a free copy of *Passing It On* or the "Mentor Orientation" from the MentorLink.org website. Then take six to twelve people through it, meeting once per week for four to six weeks. Once done, take the same group through "The Leader's Covenant," talking about and praying over one to three commitments each week until you are done.

Another resource is the MentorLink Institute. There are modules that expand the topics of grace, kingdom, leading in light of eternity, collaboration, servant leadership, and others designed for mentor groups. Each module has a "Mentee Guide" as well as a "Mentor Guide." These approaches provide starting places for anyone wanting to engage in developing leaders like Jesus did. They are ready-made approaches based on the principles in this book. There are many other approaches as well. Regardless of what you choose to do to start, I urge that you start.

You need little if any money to do this. Megaministries come and go. They raise a lot of money and have big conferences that do a little good, but when they are gone, then what? Jesus's approach uses little or no money and expands based on relationship and people's alignment with Jesus. Remember Tim and Sam? Sam's ministry died with him, while Tim's continued to multiply.

Building leaders is always in the context of relationship and life. This approach can be done from a distance as well. Consider that Paul used the latest technology of his day with the Roman transportation system and written letters. He wrote to the church in Rome, sharing his heart but never having been there. He was remote but still effective. Consider that Paul's mentoring letters to Titus and Timothy were also done from a distance. Like Paul, we need not be limited to just the people around us that we can talk to or travel to see. We have mobile phones, Skype, and other Internet-based ways to communicate with little or no cost.

**Prayer**
*Lord Jesus, you showed the priority of developing leaders while you were on earth. May I have courage and boldness to follow your model.* (Matt. 28:16–20)

**Questions for Thought or Discussion**
1. The illustration of Sam and Tim reveals many truths. How did this illustration impact you?
2. Twelve principles for developing leaders were discussed in this chapter. Which two to three principles most impacted you?
3. What steps can you take in the next two to four weeks to begin?
4. What is the Spirit saying to you from this book so far?

# Chapter 7

## The Subject We Don't Want to Talk About

Several years ago, I started asking leaders and groups in various countries this question: "When was the last time you heard a sermon or seminar on "false leaders"?

Experienced leaders from all parts of the world gave me a blank stare. "I can't remember," was the normal reply.

Then I asked, "When was the last time you talked about or taught on the topic?" They had a similar response.

Whether pastors of prominent churches, leaders of mission boards, network leaders, church planters, foundation representatives, or elders and deacons in churches, the topic is seldom, if ever, brought up. We, as leaders, seem to run from this topic. It is the subject we don't want to talk about among ourselves and the subject we rarely bring up with those we lead.

Yet Jesus made it clear what He wanted in kingdom leaders and what was not wanted. Can you imagine being a Pharisee or scribe and hearing

Jesus say, "Woe to you scribes and Pharisees, hypocrites" (Matt. 23)? He said it seven times. Jesus made it clear what He didn't want in His kingdom leaders. It made a mark on the apostles.

His apostles taught about this topic. There are many references to false leaders in the Gospels, Acts, and the Epistles. If it was such a big topic of discussion in the early church, we need to make it a common topic for ourselves and those we lead. (Note: see Appendix D for list of references). Teachings about false leaders in the New Testament serve as a warning to leaders. It clarifies what Jesus rejects.

> *Jesus will evaluate each of us based on His standards and criteria for kingdom leaders and not our own.*

There is more about what kingdom leaders are to be and not be in the New Testament than there is about "church." Consider the number of positive or negative direct teachings on leadership. How many direct teachings on "church"? Then consider that each Gospel, Acts, and Epistle was written by one of the leaders in the "church." We know what they did by what they focused on in their writings.

Something is wrong with us when we seldom raise this topic, address this issue, and take Jesus's teaching seriously. Could it be that we are not leading in light of eternity? Could it be that there are more false leaders among us than we could imagine? Could it be that we are afraid of what it will do to those who follow us if we really addressed this topic? Could it be that we don't want to lose our position or the number of followers we have? Could it be that we care more about what people think of us than what Jesus thinks of us?

## Three Kinds of False Leaders

There are many passages about false leaders in the New Testament, and there are many ways to look at this topic. I suggest that there are three ways to discern false leaders:

1. Doctrinal false leaders
2. Character false leaders
3. Ministry false leaders

This is my way of categorizing false leaders. However, at some point I suggest you do this on your own. Simply look at all the passages on false leaders in the New Testament (see Appendix D for a comprehensive list) and then summarize what you see in terms of categories that make sense to you. Then begin teaching and sharing what the Spirit taught you. I offer my thoughts to prompt further study.

Jesus will evaluate each of us based on His standards and criteria for kingdom leaders and not our own. If you are a pastor or leader of any kind of ministry, I urge you to do this study on your own. Do this for your own sake and the sake of those you influence.

## Doctrinal False Leaders

Doctrinal heresy is the most obvious way people identify a false leader. In our evangelical world, we are savvy as to what false teaching is. Seminaries, Bible colleges, and books emphasize correct doctrine. Some of the best Bible teachers are on TV, YouTube, and podcasts; write books; and are featured speakers at well-attended seminars and conferences. Also many false leaders broadcast their heresies far and wide.

Many think the only category for false leaders was the "false teacher" who taught bad doctrine. This is incomplete. Because we focus on doctrine and not on living out the Bible, we miss so much of the New Testament emphasis.

When we talk of doctrinal false teachers, we are not talking about the minor issues of the faith, such as how or when to be baptized, what kind of church governance to use, or other noncentral issues.

For several decades I have worked with leaders of churches, ministries, denominations, and mission boards from many parts of the world and from many Christian persuasions. For these many leaders who truly are concerned about the growth of the church in their nation, region, or town, there is tremendous unity. This is because we major on the majors of the faith and focus on the things that concern Jesus and His people.

Paul said,

> Preach the word…For the time will come when they will not endure sound doctrine; but wanting to have their ears tickled, they will accumulate for themselves teachers in accordance to their own desires, and will turn away their ears from the truth and will turn aside to myths. (2 Tim. 4:3–4)

It is the Word, the written Scriptures, particularly the New Testament, that is our authority for ministry and guide to how we lead, treat people, and minister in the name of Jesus and the power of the Spirit. The Scriptures are authoritative for us. To live under Jesus's authority and Lordship is to live under His Word. After all, He is the Word (John 1), and when He returns, "His name is called the Word of God" (Rev. 19:13).

Many in our day seek great numbers of followers. This is the motivation of some pastors, ministry leaders, and their boards. "Success" is demonstrated by size isn't it, they think. But in order to be attractive to so many people, they accommodate the Scriptures and make it palatable to the masses. This way of thinking is foreign to the ways of Christ and the apostles. Accommodators are really those who have historically been called "man pleasers." They are people "who loved the approval of man rather than the approval of God" (John 12:42–43).

"Man pleasers" are prevalent in our churches. They teach people to accommodate to the culture in the name of toleration. Paul warns us about these leaders who "hold to a form of godliness but have denied its power" (2 Tim. 3:5). They use God words but reject the spirit and authority of Jesus. They teach people to tolerate and even embrace cultural norms over the teachings of Jesus and His apostles. It is sobering to recall that Satan took pieces of the Bible three times to attempt to manipulate Jesus. False leaders do the same.

Jesus spoke the word (John 6) and many left. The message to God's people is a discipleship message. The message to the lost is one of salvation. The apostles taught the people of God a discipleship message— one of living, thinking, and relating to people under the Lordship of Jesus.

We need to be grounded in the faith as Paul said to Titus, "But as for you, speak the things fitting for sound doctrine" (Titus 2:1). Notice that he then focuses on character. "Older men are to be temperate, dignified, sensible, sound in faith, in love, in perseverance" (Titus 2:2).

We know so much, but living what we know is another matter. This then becomes the second reason people are false leaders—their character.

## Character False Leaders

Who is without sin? "If we say we have not sinned, we make Him a liar and His word is not in us" (1 John 1:10). The issue is not perfection in a leader but rather the state of a leader's heart, values, motives, and character.

Peter highlights character issues of false leaders in his second letter. Yes, they do introduce destructive heresies (false teaching), but their real condemnation comes from their character. He points out their shameful ways of greed, exploitation, arrogance, adulterous eyes, seduction, and reveling in their pleasures. Peter says, "These men are springs without water and mists driven by a storm. Blackest darkness is reserved for them" (2 Pet. 2:17).

*The veneer of doctrinal correctness can rot our souls. Many of us hide behind our theological systems and give little attention to pursuing godliness.*

Jesus rebuked the Pharisees and scribes repeatedly for their character. "Hypocrites" was His one-word summary. They said one thing and did another. They majored on the minors, twisted Scriptures to their own ends, and put on a show to be noticed by people thinking they would preserve their religious reputation (Matt. 23).

Jude says it differently. These false leaders creep in among us unnoticed, living undisciplined, fleshly lives. They are intentional, and their actions influence people toward themselves and their way of thinking. Rebellious and arrogant in their heart, they think they know what they really do not know. They are self-centered and ungodly in their life and with their words. They cause divisions, are worldly minded and devoid of the Spirit. They are manipulators toward their own ends and do not fear the Lord or give thought to being evaluated by Him.

### How Does This Look Today?
We are tempted to soft-pedal teaching on our human sickness—sin. In our cultures we pay a cost to claim Christ as Lord and call people to

live godly and holy lives. What if a teacher or pastor doesn't teach on sin, that Jesus is the only way, and that pure and godly living under the Lordship of Jesus is expected of His followers? Is this because the teacher might offend people and he or she is afraid they won't come back. What are his or her motives? Big crowds usually mean big budgets, big buildings, and a big salary. Though many church leaders have good hearts, some do not. Ambition can drive us to become masters of manipulation and skilled communicators, driven by greed for more and bigger.

The veneer of doctrinal correctness can rot our souls. Many of us hide behind our theological systems and give little attention to pursuing godliness. Yes, we need to understand and teach correct doctrine and at the same time pursue godly living and Christlike character. It is our character that validates our message. Paul made it clear that elders and deacons were qualified or disqualified by their character (1 Tim. 3). As Paul says, "Godliness is profitable for all things, since it holds promise for the present life and also for the life to come" (1 Tim. 4:8).

What if someone is caught in a character problem? Paul gives this direction: "Brethren, even if anyone is caught in any trespass, you who are spiritual, restore such a one in a spirit of gentleness; each one looking to yourself, so that you too will not be tempted" (Gal 6:1).

At any point in my life, I can be a false leader by my character failures. This thought drives me to rely on the grace of Jesus. "Now to Him who is able to keep you from stumbling and to make you stand in the presence of His glory, blameless with great joy…" (Jude 24).

## Ministry False Leaders
Early in my Christian life, I observed a leader who used his dominating personality to shame and subdue his followers. His approach made people timid to "challenge" him in any way. As a result he rose in his ministry organization because he was an "effective leader and got things

done." With any sensitivity and only casual observation, one could see wounded and shattered people in the wake of his influence. Jesus said, "You will know them by their fruits" (Matt. 7:15–20).

This is an example of a false leader because of his ministry approach or results. Another label is spiritual abuse. It is toxic to those under this kind of leader's influence. Those who make it out of the system often leave feeling defeated, like failures or like second-class citizens.

We are not just talking about a question of abuse. We must look at the people in a ministry over a period of time. What is the fruit coming from them? They reflect the leader's ministry. Are these people growing in expressions of the fruit of the Spirit? Are they growing in Christlikeness? Jesus said you will know them by their fruit.

How many of us have manipulated, shamed, dominated, threatened, and even fired those who didn't conform to our direction? If we are honest, most of us ministry leaders affirm that we have done some form of this at some time in our ministries. Our heart was not right at that point. Perhaps we only knew the way of the world's leadership because we weren't shown Jesus's way. Regardless of why we did it, whether in the flesh, in direct rebellion to Jesus, or even in ignorance, at that point we were false leaders because of the way we dealt with those we influenced. Perhaps we taught correct doctrine in our messages and sermons, but, still, we were false leaders because of the way we treated people.

I observed from a distance a "CEO pastor" who came into a church and decimated its core leaders and families. He did this in the name of making changes to be relevant to the lost that would come to the church. His goal was to make the church a "seeker church." Result? There were spiritual people leaving the church for years. These people came to Christ through this church. Now because of the new pastor, they were marginalized and rejected so many left.

The church was his to run and shape according to his vision.

What was the ministry outcome of his leadership? He did what he wanted and got what he asked for. He didn't seem concerned that spiritual people gave up on the church. All he seemed to care about was that the church grew numerically—and it did. He eventually got his new building on good property right off a freeway. He got his bigger numbers and his theater-quality preaching center. But at what damage to people in the process? What will those sheep he was assigned to shepherd say to Jesus? Their hurts and wounds were insignificant in importance compared to accomplishing his vision regardless of who he wounded or offended. Was he a Christlike leader? The real question is, "What will Jesus say to him when He evaluates his ministry?"

> *We read about false leaders and most of us will say, "At times, that was me." Perhaps guilt and shame are our feelings right now. I am reminded of the grace of Jesus toward the woman caught in adultery.*

We read about false leaders, and most of us will say, "At times, that was me." Perhaps guilt and shame are our feelings right now. I am reminded of the grace of Jesus toward the woman caught in adultery. Her accusers wanted to stone her. Jesus bent down and wrote in the dirt. "Let him who is without sin cast the first stone," He said to them. They all left one by one until she stood alone before Jesus. He did not condone her sin; He said, "Go and sin no more" (John 8:1–11). I am constantly amazed at Jesus's tenderness and grace with sinners and repentant people. He gives grace and forgiveness to you and me. He did not negate the seriousness of sin. Loving the sinner and hating the sin is the way of Jesus.

**Prosperity Gospel**

The prosperity gospel is a movement sweeping much of the developing world. Africa and Latin America are two areas where this movement is thriving. It is known also as the "health and wealth gospel" or the "gospel of success." It is a movement where many false leaders are evident to spiritually discerning people.

One leader in Cameroon shared with me that the prosperity gospel affects 75 percent of the leaders and churches. He said, "Pastors who want to maintain their people preach prosperity. It is what the people want to hear. It is like parents bringing candy to their children because they want it."

What Jesus values is not important, but the quantity of money you can get and give is what matters. A person's spirituality or a leader's spirituality is measured by his or her wealth and possessions."

My purpose is not to detail this false doctrine and ministry practice but to say that false-ministry practices of all kinds have popular appeal to leaders because they attract people and appeal to our comfort and pleasure. The best thing we can do to counter this and other deceptions is to train and mentor leaders in the ways of Jesus, His teaching about false leaders, and the vision to lead in light of eternity.

**How Do We Respond to False Leaders?**

Now that we are more aware of the traits and categories of false leaders, we probably know a few. What do we do with them? Perhaps even more seriously for us, we see traits of a false leader in ourselves. What do we do?

The first step for ourselves is always to turn from our fleshly or evil ways. Repentance is always first. One of the deep messages of this book is to call us to look at Jesus's standards and teaching for leaders. He wants us to turn from our fleshly, worldly ways of leading and conform to His ways. Confession, seeking forgiveness, and repentance is the process. If we each truly look at ourselves compared to Jesus's and His apostles' teachings, all of us will have some repenting to do.

What about others? Paul mentioned a false leader by name in a personal letter (Demas—2 Tim. 4:9) as did John (Diotrephes—3 John 9–11). Peter and Jude did not mention any by name in their public letters but rather by description. In His public ministry, Jesus rebuked some leaders in His presence. Everyone saw right in front of them the faces of the Pharisees and scribes present for Matthew 23. Can you imagine the rage in their hearts and on their faces at Jesus's public rebuke? He also taught about false leaders calling some Balaam, Jezebel, or Nicholatians (Rev. 2:6, 15).

*Notice Paul's grief and sorrow when he spoke of false leaders among God's people. Also note Paul's commitment to faithfully address this topic of false leaders when he spoke to the Ephesian elders for the last time.*

False leaders, particularly those with fleshly motives and character, are not always apparent. It often takes some time to see through them. As Paul said, "For some men, their sins are quite obvious, for others, they follow after" (1 Tim. 5:24). We are slow to pick up fleshly and ungodly motives and subtle ungodly character flaws because we qualify leaders by a pervasive model of content transfer. In Jesus's training of the twelve and the early apostles ministries, Christlike character was first and foremost. It must become the same for us today.

Our goal is not to eradicate false leaders. Jesus taught us not to try. In the parable of the wheat and tares (Matt 13:24–30), Jesus indicated the enemy sows tares. The temptation is to rip out tares, but Jesus says let them grow together until the harvest. At the harvest the reapers will first gather tares and burn them up but will gather wheat into His barn.

Jesus also said, "Let them alone; they are blind guides of the blind. And if a blind man guides a blind man, both will fall into a pit" (Matt. 15:14).

Notice Paul's grief and sorrow when he spoke of false leaders among God's people. Also note Paul's commitment to faithfully address this topic of false leaders when he spoke to the Ephesian elders for the last time.

> Therefore, I testify to you this day that I am innocent of the blood of all men. For I did not shrink from declaring to you the whole purpose of God. Be on guard for yourselves and for all the flock, among which the Holy Spirit has made you overseers, to shepherd the church of God which He purchased with His own blood. I know that after my departure savage wolves will come in among you, not sparing the flock; and from among your own selves men will arise, speaking perverse things, to draw away the disciples after them. Therefore be on the alert, remembering that night and day for a period of three years I did not cease to admonish each one with tears. (Acts 20:27–31)

I was in coffee a shop recently, talking with my longtime friend about this topic. He made a profound statement: "False leaders are not in the closet—it's those who are faithful who are in the closet." He is right. We need leaders working together across denominational lines to ensure false teaching isn't being propagated without a response from faithful, godly leaders. Let's get out of the closet and speak into this issue with those we influence. After all, we will stand before Jesus for our personal audit.

Several decades ago, I was an elder at a fast-growing church. We had a pastor with strong communication gifts. The church was growing quickly, and many quality spiritual leaders were joining the church. Many people were coming to Christ, but something wasn't right. A number of us elders began discussing what was going on with the pastor's character. We still couldn't put our finger on it but spent time praying and interacting. We decided to broach the subject in an elders' meeting. Our goal was to get the pastor to spend more time with his family and focus more on his own spiritual life while giving the day-to-day running of the church to his most able associate. This caused a major blowup. Since we weren't seeking to divide the church in any way, we elders who saw this (almost half of the elder board) quietly left the elder board and the church over the next year or so.

About three years later, the pastor was caught in sexual indiscretion. Everything exploded, and the church was in crisis over this pastor's refusal to take a leave of absence to work on his character and marriage. After seeking many ways to address the issue to bring healing to the pastor, he was finally fired. Many were deeply hurt. It is hard to imagine a false leader right in our midst who influenced us each week.

Perhaps Jude's words best summarize how we should respond to false leaders: "Have mercy on some, who are doubting; save others, snatching them out of the fire; and on some have mercy with fear, hating even the garment polluted by the flesh" (Jude 22–23).

Should we shrink back because we are afraid of being a false leader? By all means don't do this. Instead "be steadfast, immovable, always abounding in the work of the Lord, knowing that your toil is not in vain in the Lord" (1 Cor. 15:58).

Jesus, the high, exalted Creator; King; and Savior of the world, went down into the Jordan River to be baptized by John. John was shocked. Jesus should be exalted. John knew he was not even worthy to untie Jesus's sandals and did not want to identify Jesus with repentance and forgiveness of sins (Matt. 3). But Jesus did this to identify with us. We have a great High Priest and Mediator who understands our weaknesses. He loves and intercedes for us.

"Now to Him who is able to keep you from stumbling and to make you stand in the presence of His glory blameless with great joy, to the only God our Savior, through Jesus Christ our Lord, be glory, majesty, dominion and authority, before all time and now and forever. Amen" (Jude 24–25).

**Prayer**
*Lord, from my heart, I want to be a faithful undershepherd of Your people. Open my eyes to where I've been a false leader in any way. Teach me Your ways. Show me Your truth, and lead me by Your Spirit so I can faithfully serve You and Your people.* (Psalm 25:4–5)

**Questions for Thought or Discussion**
1. Look through the list of Scriptures in Appendix D. What observations do you make?
2. How did this chapter make you feel?

3. Look over the types of false leaders in this chapter. Which ones have you personally observed in others?
4. What are some areas in your life, leading, or ministry that the Spirit convicted you of?

# Chapter 8

## ORGANIZATIONALISM—A PERVASIVE IDOL

I approach this chapter with some anxiety. I am afraid that you will misunderstand or I will be misunderstood. I am concerned that the issues will be glossed over, the seriousness of the issues lost. I also approach this chapter with much thought, counsel, and prayer. I am attempting to put in words what I've not read anywhere, but it is the air we breathe.

I was on Navigator staff from 1976 until 2000 with many responsibilities and ministry experiences. Throughout my Christian life, I've been mentored by some of the best mentors available to me—many of them senior Navigators. These were men I highly respected for their godliness, wisdom, and experience. Without the input of these men, I couldn't or wouldn't be doing what I do. I stand on their shoulders, and I am deeply grateful for their love, grace, and patience with me.

While on Navigator staff, I led a campus ministry and a community ministry, I was founder of the Glen Eyrie Leadership Development Institute, and I participated in many US and some international projects. As a Navigator I was tasked as executive director of the CoMission Training and Materials Committee (1992–1997) where the CoMission partnership of eighty-four denominations and mission organizations sent 1,868 missionaries for at least a year to sixty-eight cities in the former Soviet Union. The Lord expanded and honed my gifts of developing people, providing leadership, building teams, and building organizations. As I write these words, I see pictures of many who are now champions of the faith in their careers, churches, ministries, and families. I keep up with some and occasionally hear about others. I feel privileged to have had a small part in their growth and development.

In 1997 the US Navigators began a process to select a new president. At that time the president was responsible for twenty-five hundred staff. I was a candidate. There were thirty-nine members of a committee who would select the new president over two separate five-day meetings.

As the final week progressed, there were two of us remaining. Several votes were taken, but the results were about even, and neither of us had the 75 percent required votes needed. Late on day four, we held another vote, and there were a few more votes for the other man but still less than the required 75 percent—we had run out of time and were scheduled to conclude our meeting by midmorning the next day.

That night was a sleepless one for me. Somewhere in the middle of the night, I knew God wanted me to withdraw my name. The other man was then the clear choice to be the president.

The next morning I got up from my table and walked a short distance to the podium and spoke briefly to the other thirty-eight men and women in the room. I shared only briefly and said in essence, "I withdraw." As soon as I said these words, I broke down weeping on the verge of collapse. Some nearby helped me to my seat.

I went home knowing I had done the right thing. But I've never been so broken, defeated, and abandoned or felt so rejected. These thirty-eight other men and women respected me, loved me, and did not reject me. It was nothing they did or didn't do. It was me and what God was doing in my life. Though I knew better, what I felt was deep rejection. The Navigators were my family. They led me to Christ. Where did I go from here?

Over the next year, I spiraled downward, losing both perspective and vision. I did little constructive. The new president graciously provided a resource person, who formed a "protection team" for me. The idea was that these people would be a sounding board for me as I journeyed through these deep waters. I look back now and realize the Lord used these men to rescue me.

The Lord orchestrated these events for many reasons— one was my growth. One of

*What I am illustrating is the subtle, sneaky drift in our lives as leaders. We come to shape our identity around the group we are with and where we fit in the group. We fall in love with the system of ministry. The desire to be on the inner circles is a strong one.*

the hardest parts was that I lost my ability to sense what God was doing in my life. I remember saying, "I don't trust myself to listen to the Lord anymore." It seemed like God led me in the direction of leading this organization and then abruptly shut the door. I was lost.

I slowly began to see how I had fused my vision to a position and an organization. I saw my dependency on the significance of my position in the organization and my desire to be in the inner circle. I saw that my significance, my identity, came from being on the inside and on top. This dies slow.

I am grateful the Lord gave the responsibility to the other man. He did a great job for eleven years. I am deeply thankful to the Lord for the brokenness that He brought in me through this experience. I have no residual hurt or rejection. My identity in Christ has grown significantly. I am so thankful for the way the Lord used all of this to prepare me for the next chapter of my life and ministry, which began in 2000 when God called me to help form MentorLink.

The point in sharing this breaking experience in my life is to illustrate how much organizational cultures have been part of my life.

What I am illustrating is the subtle, sneaky drift in our lives as leaders. We come to shape our identity around the group we are with and where we fit in the group. We fall in love with the system of ministry. The desire to be on the inner circles is a strong one.

In the world of vocational ministry, we don't drive company cars or get a yearly bonus. No one enters the ministry for the perks. A dangerous temptation is to wrap our soul around the job we do, the organization we are a part of, the position we hold, or the staff and budgets we control. C. S. Lewis calls this in his timeless essay, the longing to be in the inner ring.

> Of all passions the passion for the Inner Ring is more skillful in making a man who is not yet a very bad man do bad things… The desire to be inside the invisible line illustrates this rule. As long as you are governed by that desire you will never get what you want. You are trying to peel an onion; if you succeed there will be nothing left. Until you conquer the fear of being an

outsider, an outsider you will remain. (C. S. Lewis, *The Weight of Glory*, "The Inner Ring," p. 103)

## Organizations

This is very important: this chapter is not about The Navigators or any other specific organization or church. It is about the organizational air we breathe and the temptation we all face to use organizations for our own fleshly desires. Like the polluted air in Beijing is hazardous to our physical health, organizations can be hazardous to our spiritual health.

> *Though our heart is good, our actions sometimes reveal we are organizationally focused and our organizational focus takes precedence over Jesus and His kingdom. This is idolatry.*

Most of us in ministry organizations and churches have good hearts and are not seeking to undermine the kingdom. Perhaps at times we know something is wrong or that what we do is not from the pages of the New Testament, but we are carried along by the momentum of the organization. Perhaps we don't like how the organization treats people but "godly" leaders above us do it, other ministries and churches do it, and we just assume those people are right. Though our heart is good, our actions sometimes reveal we are organizationally focused and our organizational focus takes precedence over Jesus and His kingdom. This is idolatry.

Organizations are neutral—they are wineskins. They are containers or structures around some idea or activity. Wikipedia defines it this way:

> An organization is a social entity that has a collective goal and is linked to an external environment. The word is derived from the Greek word organon, itself derived from the better-known word ergon which means "organ"—a compartment for a particular task.

"An organization is a social entity…" we build around a purpose or task. The key point is that it is a structure that helps people relate and work together.

Structure is needed to support life. We have skin and bones. Flowers have stalks, and trees have trunks and branches. The solar system has structure. This chapter is not about doing away with organizations.

As I write, we are in December and our home is decorated for Christmas. Soon all will be here for three to four days of joy and celebration of His greatest gift. I am sitting in front of our fireplace with the gas logs burning and the threat of the pending ice storm showing in the gray clouds through the window behind me. The fire is in the fireplace. This is right and safe. The fire has a purpose of warmth and ambiance and if in the right place, serves that purpose well. Warmth is produced and gentle sounds of the fire and dancing flames provide a great Christmas-like atmosphere I enjoy on this cold winter's day. If there were no container or fireplace, what would happen if there was a fire in our house?

Structure is part of the way our God holds creation together. It is what we do with ministry structures in the name of God that can become the issue. Ministry structures and systems can actually become idols.

Organizations in the Body of Christ can fall under the control of fleshly people who use it for their own ends. Manipulation, abuse of power, and control over people can be justified under the mandates of the organization. The organization becomes the centerpiece or focal point and takes authority away from Jesus. It is a way leaders get away with fleshly practices. This is what I call organizationalism.

## Organizationalism Illustrated

Organizationalism is where the organization is the focal point. Rather than attempting to conceptually explain it, let's illustrate it.

Organizationalism as an idol was first seen in Genesis 11 with the tower of Babel. People said, "Come, let us build for ourselves a city, and a tower whose top will reach into heaven, and let us make for ourselves a name, otherwise we will be scattered abroad over the face of the whole earth" (Gen. 11:4). God confused their speech from that experience and scattered them as peoples and nations over the earth. They focused on their structure with the motive to make a name for themselves.

Have you ever been in one of the beautiful church buildings in Europe? They represent phenomenal artistic and architectural accomplishments. They took decades to build. What were their motives? The Lord knows. People must have been proud of them. To this day they are beautiful. They are monuments of massive financial investments in their construction. But they were never the true church in that area. The true church, the Body of Christ, is the people. We lose sight of this and give prominence to buildings instead. The people are gone, but the monument remains with us. We often do a variation of this when we place focus on our organization's name or logo. People come and go, yet the organization remains—we forget the original purpose of the building or organization and instead honor the building or organizational remnants.

I recently did an enlightening study looking at the strategies and practices of the Pharisees and Chief Priests in the Gospels. This is a worthy study if you want to see organizationalism in operation (see Appendix D for a list of references). Their power and authority was undermined when Jesus and His followers did not bow to their system of rules and regulations or their authority. So they attacked Him, tried to trap, shame and undermine Him using any means possible. Their system, role and power depended on their control. These 'spiritual leaders' in Jesus' day manipulated the crowds to get Jesus crucified. They were protecting their system and organizational status quo. This is organizationalism.

Jesus means to be the focus of people's attention. The Pharisees rejected this notion when they said, "If we let Him go on like this, all men will believe in Him, and the Romans will come and take away both our place and our nation" (John 11:48). They were solid in their positions and place in the system they built. They liked their identity. They were fearful at the possibility of losing it. This is the root of the problem they and we face. We desire a name for ourselves and the place we built. Jesus will challenge this in each of us. He will be the focal point and will not share His glory with another.

They guarded their positions. It was not about the good things Jesus did like the many He healed, the demons He cast out, the miracles He performed, or the lives He changed. It was about their system and control.

Jesus gives a strong word of warning: "Watch out and beware of the leaven of the Pharisees and Sadducees" (Matt. 16:6). Each one of us in leadership ought to be sobered by this warning. The question is, "Am I like the Pharisees and Sadducees in any way?"

**Current Examples**
Let's look at some illustrations of organizationalism in action today:

### 1. Changing Strategy
A megachurch decided to change strategies of structure and ministry. Their move is toward only small groups because this is "the way __(name)__ [a well-known pastor in the United States] has organized his

church." Seems innocent to say there is a change of strategy. Also it seems innocent to build the church structure around small groups.

This change raises motivation questions: Are people actually being served by this change? Who do the leaders serve?

This change abandoned many effective ministries in order to incorporate the new strategy. "We want to eliminate all programs and go to small groups," is what was said. What about the very fruitful men's discipling ministry or other groups that were canceled?

When we announce a new strategy that is an effort to copy a "successful" ministry, we are in danger of succumbing to organizationalism. It is as though numerical growth was the sole goal, like a beast that must be fed. Where is the leading of God?

Behind this action is the assumption that organizational alignment, structural management, and conformity of people in small groups will grow the church. Is this assumption correct? Is this really true? What are the motives? Who wants this most of all? The pastor? Will organizational realignment really bring about growth in the heart, values, motives, and character of the people the leaders are supposed to serve?

Organizationalism can become the prominent paradigm of ministry, like the proverbial tail that wags the dog. It takes precedence over spiritual means given us. The path slowly but surely takes us away from what is central, what is important. It is vital to note here that the apostles delegated administrative tasks to spiritual men (Philip and Stephen, Acts 6–7) who did not lead with their administrative gifts and skills but rather from their prime focus on spiritual tools centered in Jesus.

It is also vital for us to note that Jesus severely rebuked the scribes and Pharisees for their organizationalism (Matt. 23 and other places). This ought to serve as a warning to each of us who lead existing organizations. If we are not careful, we can find ourselves opposing Jesus.

## 2. Protecting the Leader's Turf

Leaders use organizations to protect their turf or empire. Two veteran missionaries are kept out of a large city because a leader was threatened by their presence. "They aren't controllable," he says. This man used this statement to keep many other national and expat missionaries out of "his area" over the years. But now his peers see that he has used this same strategy to remove others or prevent missionaries from coming in. "Deceptive and manipulative" are words that describes his control over the organization, but on the outside he kept up a good front, using all the right language. This is beneath our calling as leaders who are mandated to help fulfill the Great Commission in our world.

## 3. New Leader—New Conformity

There was a missionary who had proven effectiveness in a nation. A new leader was appointed to oversee the organization's national ministry. This new boss came in, looked at the veteran missionary's ministry, and said in essence, "You are not doing what we want, so you must leave."

As soon as I heard this, I called him since he was a longtime friend. I asked, "What is your calling?" I said, "Find another wineskin that will allow you to do your calling." In time he and his wife found another organization and returned to the nation with a very fruitful ministry.

This illustrates the issue. Some leaders are threatened when God uses a person outside their control and direction. This is organizationalism. We have put the organization ahead of what the Spirit is doing through a person, group, or ministry. This is the leader saying "I am lord," "do what I say," and "I am in control here." In ministry we are not given company cars, expense accounts, or extended vacations. To compensate we fall to the temptation to feed our ego on position and control. But the cause of Christ suffers.

### *4. An African Perspective*
I asked several ministry leaders from Africa about this issue. They said, "Leaders protect their empire. The name of the organization or church is more important than Jesus's kingdom. They produce only leaders like themselves. There is a high level of corruption among these leaders because they have to grow their ministry. So they manipulate people and use the 'prosperity gospel' message to get people to come to their church and give money. People in the ministry see this and begin to do the same. Younger leaders observe and try to follow their model. The goal is to grow the leader's ministry, not the kingdom of Jesus."

The African scene is raw, but much the same happens everywhere. Paul addressed the carnal Corinthian church, which had divided into different camps. "'I am of Paul,' and 'I of Apollos,' and 'I of Cephas,' and 'I of Christ'" (I Cor. 1:12). Paul rebuked this approach of dividing loyalties with Christ by focusing on well-known leaders. This is alive and well in our day with our organizational divisions. The focal point is not Jesus and his kingdom but rather man-made structures or charismatic leaders.

### *5. Handling Missions Giving in a Church*
With the proliferation of mission organizations and ministries at local, national, and international levels, churches are tempted to focus only on the ones they own and control. Larger churches set up their own mission board and send out their own missionaries. The message comes from many pulpits: "Give your money to us, and we will distribute it to the missions and ministries we authorize." What are the motives? More churches than can be imagined have even reduced or canceled missions giving to redirect the funds to build bigger buildings and expand the organization and ministries to church members and attendees. What

are the motives? What is in the heart of the decision makers? How will Jesus evaluate this?

### 6. Focusing on Market Share and Distinctiveness

Seeking a "competitive edge" for increased market share is a driving force in our economically driven world. In the business world, we gain market share by focusing on our distinctives; by marketing our products and services; and by cutting poor producers, including products, services, and people. In ministries we often do the same as we seek to grow our ministry. The focus is on organizational growth using business-world principles.

These principles work—just look at Coca-Cola, Apple, McDonald's, and many other successful enterprises. We are not challenging their use in the business world. But what happens when these principles are applied to churches and ministries? What damage does this do to the weak, downcast, and marginalized?

The fellow citizens in the church are primarily a family. We are relationally connected. Leaders and influencers among His saints are called brothers, fellow workers, friends, servants, and a host of other relationally oriented words (see Appendix C for a graphic illustrating this). The driving values of a healthy family are love, building one another up, and co-operation among the members. This is not "competitive edge" thinking.

Ministries and churches that focus on themselves and their "competitive edge" and uniqueness will, by default, seek to build themselves up while putting others down either inadvertently or intentionally. The focus is on the organization and not Jesus. What does Jesus think of this?

### Organizationalism Summary

Organizations apply form to function to get things done. Organizations allow us to maximize scarce people, money, and time resources.

Segregation of duties, utilizing strengths of people, financial efficiencies of scale, and collective understanding of organizational goals can lead to maximizing people and resources. This can be of great value to the organization's purposes.

Good things can transform into bad things. Organizationalism can have disastrous consequences. Organizationalism is when we cede power and allegiance to the organization run by its leaders. The leaders become pawns of higher leaders or of the historical system and end up doing things they question or feel uncomfortable with from a kingdom perspective. Leaders can use the organization for their own purposes, manipulating people and resources toward their own ends. First and foremost, the organization is key and at the center of activity and thought. Second, leaders, managers, or pastors subtly take control, eliminating threats to their agenda, power, or position.

Where is the Trinity in a practical day-to-day way? How does the Spirit move? Who is head of the Body? Who is sovereign over all the organizational goals?

There are false leaders, emotionally disturbed people, and secret disrupters. Jesus, Paul, Peter, Jude, and John inform us that they are there, and they want to disrupt a ministry, seek control of it, or undermine the work of Jesus in some way for their own dark motives. There are ways to handle these, but organizationalism is not the answer. Just letting them corrupt the work of God is not the answer either. Sometimes they need to be confronted by name. Sometimes they need to be removed from their positions and have their relationships severed. Things are not clean-cut, clear, or without emotional and sometimes financial costs.

Sometimes the effort to reorganize a ministry or streamline for effectiveness can be a clever means of consolidating power. We need to evaluate our motives and prayerfully consider what God is doing in our midst.

Structure must follow what the Spirit is doing in and through people. Structures and organizations must serve Christ's people not the other way around.

Most of us appreciate a smooth-running organization and people working together efficiently, but sometimes the Spirit pulls people away and does unexpected things with genuine fruit. We can't control it—only serve those involved, and join in what the Spirit is doing. The ultimate goal is not a smooth-running organization but rather serving what the Spirit is doing. If we can't serve it, perhaps the Spirit is breaking out a new ministry.

What can we do if we are in an environment of organizationalism? Here are some thoughts:

*If You Are the Leader*
- If at any point, you see that you are opposing Jesus by leading or living in the flesh, confess this sin.
- Review this book, and ask the Lord what actions He wants you to take.
- Take a number of leaders you influence through this book and after you finish, ask the group to seek the Lord for the actions He wants you to take.
- Ask the Spirit to hold you by the hand and lead you in the steps you need to take in courage, faith, and boldness.

*If You Are Not the Leader*
- Pioneer a new expression, but don't split the old wineskin. This may be perceived as rebellion by organizational thinkers. Sometimes pioneering is not rebellion but rather obedience.
- Do nothing but keep your distance from the center of the organization.

- Commit to reform the organization. This is a long-term project. You must be called to this because it will be very costly.
- Join another like-minded organization or church. Most will take this approach because in the short run, it will be a breath of fresh air. This is often why people leave one church or ministry and go to another.

If we've been wounded by organizationalism, we can learn much about God's sovereign watch-care over us by looking at Joseph. His jealous brothers sold him into slavery attempting to rid themselves of him and his status as their father's favorite son. We see Joseph's response when his brothers feared retribution for their actions: "You meant evil against me, but God meant it for good…" (Gen. 50:20). Yes, even though leaders or organizations abuse or mistreat us, God can still use it in our lives for His purposes.

## Antidotes to Organizationalism

### My Own Journey
We made partnerships one of our key operating values and strategies when we formed MentorLink. We did this the best we knew how. We grew rapidly by serving as catalysts to help known leaders in a country form a mentoring network to develop leaders. We trained key leaders in a five-day-retreat format, gave them initial materials, and told them these materials were not completely right for their context. We encouraged them to modify the materials as they felt needed. We also gave all the participants the electronic files of the materials on a CD so they could easily make the contextual modifications. Then we viewed them as partners in the overall MentorLink movement. This was going well. In seven years we were in over twenty nations.

As we grew, we started giving titles and looking more like an organization. Even though we called them partners, we began falling into management mode. They were kind and in some ways went along with this.

Then 2008 hit. We had just brought in my replacement to serve as the president of MentorLink International in February 2008 "to take the organization to the next level." I was to serve as chairman with a focus on fundraising, mentoring, and training. Things were going well. Our gift income was increasing, and our board and staff were excited. Then in May a potential donor slated to give a large gift suddenly died, one of our key staff abruptly resigned in July, and the economy crashed in August. Then my replacement unexpectedly resigned in September. So I came back to lead the MentorLink ministry. We had no money (a 66 percent decline in gifts in fifteen months because most of our large donors were connected to the real estate and financial markets) and no real organization to promote other than a few of us Americans. I told the board that when I came back in, we would stay on the edge of innovation—this was the only way to keep me energized.

> *All we had were our values, vision, and relationships, yet the ministry continued to multiply. This is counterintuitive to the organizational mind (including mine at the time).*

There were many dark nights during that period through 2011. I learned many personal, leadership, and ministry lessons in that three-year period. We struggled financially as a ministry. Organizational thinking goes like this: "I need to manage and create growth by allocating financial resources to the right people and programs." We had no money for people or programs. What were we to do?

There is something to be said for having too few resources. The ministry was forced to grow by values, vision, and relationships. It was humbling and amazing at the same time.

Through this dark phase (organizationally speaking), we continued praying for key people through our weekly e-mail prayer update. We continued to meet people from around the world in Skype groups. We also continued to create new resource materials to give away to any who would use them.

To our amazement the overall movement continued to grow and multiply.

I learned that movements can grow with little money and programs from a central source. All we had were our values, vision, and relationships, yet the ministry continued to multiply. This is counterintuitive to the organizational mind (including mine at the time). The fewer resources you throw at it, the more it grows. Who gets the glory? Not me or MentorLink.

Again, the issue is not "organization" per se. Organizations are only wineskins. They exist to serve a purpose, but they are not the purpose. As I look at the ways of Jesus and the early church, there is limited use of formalized wineskins. The Roman culture was extremely organized, yet the early church did not model its wineskins after the Roman model. This held true until Constantine married the church to the state in AD 313. Ever since then, clergy increased in power, structures increased in prominence, "lay people" diminished in power, and women lost ministry impact and influence.

If we long to see the Gospel of Christ reach the nations, we will have to de-emphasize our structures and empower average, called people to minister according to their gifts and calling.

## 4-M Chronology

Man, movement, management, and monument. Looking at a long-term perspective of church history, we see a general trend. Even looking at the last fifty years of church history, we see aspects of the general trend. It is this: God uses a person to create a ministry out of nothing or adopt a new form of ministry in a new way or to new people. Spontaneous spiritual growth happens and spreads rapidly and with little effort. Others pick it up and emulate it. This leads to multiplication. Then people run into problems, sense a need to bring order, structure or control to the growth. Management then becomes the focus.

Different kinds of leaders rise to the top of the movement who see the problems and attempt to solve them in an orderly way. This initially brings comfort to many people wanting order and structure. There is also an attempt to create formulas, programs, and materials to replicate the movement with other people. This goes on for years or decades, and new generations of managers come in. Things become routine and the spark is gone, but the ministry continues. Some managers try to renew the original spark through organizational change, management change, or programs attempting to bring revival to the ministry.

Over time people get worn out, and new generations of leaders and managers emerge who did not know the original man or movement. The only thing they know is the perceived effectiveness of the organization and point to management as the key. This goes on for years or decades. The result is a monument.

The management phase is most dangerous to the work of the Spirit in a movement. Many leaders start with the management phase. They ask these questions: What is your structure? Who are your leaders? What is your strategy? What is your vision? The attempt is to put together the best organization possible, and in doing so, they think they are expanding the ministry.

The management phase usually comes after first-generation leaders transfer the ministry to the second generation and then from the second to the third and fourth. Usually by the fourth, the ministry is in the hands of managers who are "hired" to preserve the forms and traditions of the past. The succeeding generations lose sight of the difference between function and form.

Managers celebrate the virtues of a smooth-running ministry machine and provide a continual supply of parts for the assembly line of ministry production. But a movement is like a living organism. Organisms defy outside management. If we try to organize a movement, we will kill it.

**What Fosters Movements**
We have talked at length about organizationalism, but what are some antidotes? I believe partnerships are a practical way forward. Our experience in MentorLink led us to work with partners who have a kingdom agenda larger than themselves and that seek to accomplish that agenda with partners. If a leader or organization is unwilling to partner in some aspects of their ministry, they are building their own "empire" and are not the kind of leader or organization we want to be associated with anyway. These partnerships can become a movement.

Movements are the way of the Spirit and antidotes to organizationalism. Movements happen when people, particularly gifted "apostles" are released to innovate and follow the Spirit's lead in new ways or new places of ministry.

Movements are spontaneous, widespread manifestations, implemented in a variety of methods and leaders. Think of the Orality movement, which consists of people and ministries seeking to get the Gospel and the Scriptures to two-thirds of the world that does not read. Leader development, spiritual direction, and saturation church planting movements are all current illustrations.

There are three indicators of spiritual movements: they multiply spiritual fruit, they have many leaders, and their organizations and expressions and are being used by God to change lives.

Spiritual movements grow by the work of the Spirit. Our role is to create environments that are conducive to spontaneous growth. But we cannot manufacture a movement. However, we can focus on meeting real needs and use spiritual tools of prayer, the Scriptures, and the love of Christ to serve people in need, but it is the Spirit that gives growth. Then we watch where the Spirit of God is moving, and we follow that trail.

Though we cannot manufacture movements, we can kill them through fearful or threatened leaders who desire to control outcomes and fruit. Another movement killer is the attempt to monetize the movement through charging for services. Leaders, organizations, or churches with cultures of control can kill movements.

These are decisions each leader must make:

1. Am I willing to submit to Jesus's rule in my leadership?
2. Am I willing to partner with other leaders and ministries for specific ministries?
3. Am I willing to let go of control?
4. Am I willing to not get the credit?
5. Am I willing to encourage other expressions of similar ministry?

## Summary

Structures are a part of life. Functions need forms, and forms can become organizations. Organizations are created to serve the people in a ministry or church. But they can become dominant and reverse the purpose so that the people end up serving the organization. This is called organizationalism.

Everywhere, the pressure for leaders is to build their organizations. They are held accountable to this end. Ministry leaders and pastors have a difficult time seeing another way of leading. They are often imprisoned by their organizational mandates and roles. Organizationalism is pervasive in our day. An idol is anything we give allegiance to over Jesus and His kingdom rule.

The apostle John said, "Children, guard yourselves from idols."

## Prayer

*Lord, give me eyes to see how I have bought into organizationalism and the courage to realign myself with You and Your kingdom.* (1 John 5:21)

## Questions for Thought or Discussion

1. How have you seen organizationalism expressed in your experience?
2. What movement have you been a part of or seen from a distance? What is happening to it now?
3. What is the Spirit saying to you from this chapter?

# Chapter 9

## SEVEN REALITIES FOR KINGDOM LEADERS

In this chapter we provide a seven-point summary of the book.

There are so many needs in our communities, nations, and world that cry out for the touch of Jesus. His people are called to move toward these needs as His hands and feet. Jesus calls us who are His leaders in workplaces, churches, ministries, neighborhoods, schools, and networks to lead in a different way with different realities.

Government, political, educational, and business leaders all have ways to accomplish their agendas and proven means to "move people" in their intended direction. If people don't move, they use more forceful means. We see it all around us.

Many ministry leaders, boards, financial givers, and members think the world's kind of leadership is permitted in churches, missions, and ministries—but only if it is done with a kinder face and approach than practiced in the culture around them. Is it really?

Leading in the kingdom is not the same as leading in any other aspect of culture. It is wholly different at its core and in its motives, values, and perspective.

> *Leading in the kingdom is not the same as leading in any other aspect of culture. It is wholly different at its core and in its motives, values, and perspective.*

Jesus came preaching a new reality—the kingdom. This came to a people who were under the law. As Dallas Willard says, "What had come to be understood as the Law and the Prophets in the hands of religious authorities was not the law at all, but arrangements which people in religious power had developed for crushing the life out of the citizens—general people of God—and allowing them—the leaders—to exalt themselves" (Dallas Willard, "Acts of Incarnation," *Conversations*, Vol. 11.1, pp. 20–26).

### Seven Realities

Jesus came preaching a new reality for the people of God and their leaders. While we could say much about the new reality, we want to focus on what the kingdom means for leaders. When Jesus came, He modeled and taught at least seven realities relevant for leaders in His kingdom.

1. Success Redefined
2. Upside-Down Leaders Required
3. Evaluation Criteria Clarified
4. Eternal-Reward System Revealed
5. Multiplying Leaders Modeled
6. Focused Action Mandated
7. No Exemptions

## Success Redefined

Join a group of ministry leaders, and listen to our conversations like a fly on the wall. What do we talk about? Somewhere in most conversations, we work in a brief discussion on the size of our buildings, budgets, and programs and the number of people attending our programs. Our concern is how many, how big, how fast, and how much. All these are externals by which we compare ourselves one to another. They are mere shadows of reality. If we are honest, most of us are tempted by these comparisons and tangible measures of our worth.

Who has the biggest church or ministry in your city or nation? Is he or she a success in Jesus's kingdom? Consider that Satan himself has many followers. Does the number of followers and size of buildings and budgets mean any more than Satan's? The issue is allegiance and faithfulness to the King and His kingdom.

> *Success is what Jesus says it is. After all, He is Lord.*

We fall into this trap as we relate to ministry leaders, assigning higher respect for those with bigger ministries. Success for most of us is evaluated by externals: what we can see, feel, touch, measure, analyze, and evaluate.

What does Jesus value? What does He teach about successful leaders in His kingdom? Here are a few traits and qualities of success from Jesus and His apostles:

- Humility
- Counting others as more important
- Being a servant of all

- Abiding in the vine
- Walking in the Spirit
- Encouraging, imploring, and exhorting people to follow Jesus in faithfulness
- Dying to our self, taking up our cross, and following Jesus
- Making disciples
- Equipping saints for the work of ministry
- Loving one another

Success is what Jesus says it is. After all, He is Lord. Success in His kingdom is not what our flesh wants or our Christian culture values. Successful leaders in Jesus's kingdom may not be successful in many of our religious organizations, churches, or programs. Conversely, many who are successful in our churches and ministries may not be successful in Jesus's eyes.

We need to think of success as faithfulness to Jesus and his call on our lives. Success for each of us is different because Jesus made each of us with unique gifts, callings, stewardships, resources, backgrounds, and talents. For one person called by Jesus to a global-mission organization, success is one thing; for another called to his or her own culture to serve as an elder or pastor, success will be something else. To another called to be a Daniel, Esther, or Joseph in his or her culture, success is different. Jesus's parable of the talents reveals this reality (Matt 25:15–30).

We will not know in this life the degree of our success in Jesus's eyes. We will find that out later. This we do know: a life where we strive to please Jesus will be rewarded. "Well done, good and faithful servant" are the words most of us want to hear.

### Upside-Down Leaders Required
The twelve regularly discussed among themselves who was the greatest. Who would be Jesus's second in command in the kingdom? Their

concept of the kingdom was "of this world." They assumed Jesus was coming to overthrow the Roman rulers and set up an earthly, political, visible, powerful government from which He would rule in righteousness as promised to King David.

> *Jesus's way is not a different style of leadership—it is wholly different in self-identity, motives, values, and agendas.*

With this view of the coming kingdom, they assumed that leaders would be like leaders in other governments. We know this because of numerous conversations recorded in the Gospels where the twelve discussed "who was greatest" (e.g., Mark 10). In one of these, James and John came to Jesus asking Him to seat them one on his right and one on his left in his kingdom. He refused to do this. The other ten burned with anger.

What strikes me is how deep-seated this desire for greatness was. So deep was this drive that even during the Last Supper, after He had instituted the bread and the cup and said He would be betrayed by one of them, "there arose also a dispute among them as to which one of them was regarded to be greatest." At the Last Supper, Jesus made it very clear what kind of leaders will be esteemed and honored in His kingdom.

> He said, "The kings of the Gentiles lord it over them and those who have authority over them are called 'Benefactors.' But it is not this way with you, but the one who is the greatest among you must become like the youngest, and the leader like the servant." (Luke 22:24–26)

The kingdom of God is different from the kingdoms of the world, which ultimately come under the ruler of the world, Satan himself.

The kingdoms of the world have a clear leadership paradigm. Power, control, force, manipulation, threats, and even charisma are used to maintain control and accomplish the ambitions of leaders. This is how leadership was understood then and now. We only have to read a newspaper most any day to see current examples.

Jesus's way is not a different style of leadership—it is wholly different in self-identity, motives, values, and agendas. Jesus did not use the word "servant" like so many Christian writers and most all secular writers use it today as a nicer, kinder way for the leader to control people to accomplish the leader's agenda. "Servant leadership" is popular in ministry and business worlds as a better way to lead people. This may be good, but unless Christian writers and business writers understand and promote Jesus's principles of dying to self, taking up one's cross, and following Jesus, they are promoting just another style of power leadership for the organization and leader to accomplish their goals.

Though we haven't developed it in this book, there are passive leaders who refuse to take initiative out of their own insecurity or, in some cases, hide behind the term "servant leadership." To these people these words of Paul are instructive: "For God has not given us a spirit of timidity, but of power and love and discipline" (2 Tim 1:7). Be salt and light to the world around us was Jesus's instruction.

Ask yourself these questions: Whom do I view as leaders in my church and ministries I relate to? Why do I view them as leaders? Who do I view as a successful ministry leader? Why do I view this person this way? Are my answers to these questions more like the disciples understanding or Jesus's? His is an upside-down kingdom.

**Evaluation Criteria Clarified**

Jesus is Lord. He is the One who will evaluate leaders in His kingdom. He made it clear what He wants from leaders. He also made it clear what He rebukes and rejects in leaders. Think of Peter and how he felt when Jesus said, "Get behind me, Satan. For you are not setting your mind on God's interests but man's." The disciples watching this must have had their mouths drop open. Peter thought he was doing Jesus a favor by looking out for Jesus's personal well-being and safety. Yet Peter was really looking out for his own well-being and future role in the political government the twelve expected Jesus to set up when he would overthrow the Roman oppressors (Matthew 16:21–27). Jesus rebuked Peter's self-serving motives.

The externals no longer have bearing in Jesus's kingdom. Pharisees and other religious leaders of Jesus's day wore their credentials on their ornate clothes. They prayed long prayers and went through elaborate rituals in their giving, praying, and religious ceremonies. These lived for accolades and praise from people. Jesus said they have their reward in full.

If it is not the externals, then what are the criteria? Jesus looks at the heart, values, motives, and character. He looks at how we invest our lives. He evaluates what we do in secret. He evaluates what we invest ourselves in and who we influence for His kingdom. He looks at our faithfulness to Him, His kingdom, those He calls us to serve. "For God sees not as man sees, for man looks at the outward appearance, but the Lord looks at the heart" (1 Sam 16:7).

Jesus's evaluation criteria are the opposite of the world's criteria for leaders. His is an upside-down kingdom.

**Eternal-Reward System Revealed**

"He who abides in Me and I in him, he bears much fruit, for apart from Me, you can do nothing" (John 15:5). Because we are citizens of a new kingdom, we have been grafted into the vine and adopted into the line of promises and covenants for the saints. We no longer are rewarded based on the principles of this world.

When you and I trust Jesus by His grace, we are made new. We died to the elementary principles of this world and were raised in Christ in the newness of life. Living into this eternal reality in this life is what Jesus rewards.

It is no longer what we see, measure, or define in tangible terms in this life that counts. Rather it is what Jesus sees us do in faith; in the power of the Spirit; in secret; and in our hearts, character, values, and motives.

People look on the outward appearance, but God looks at the heart. It is not eternally relevant what our earthly net worth was when we stand before Jesus. But Jesus is pleased when we give sacrificially to His causes—this builds up our eternal treasures and rewards. It is not eternally relevant how big my house is, but Jesus is pleased when we live for Him and invest in kingdom causes with our time, resources, and talent. This brings His praise and eternal rewards. It means a lot to fellow ministry leaders how big our budget and buildings are and how broad our ministry influence is, but it doesn't to Jesus. He evaluates based on His criteria.

When Jesus evaluates my life, do I want lasting rewards? Sure, most anyone reading this book wants that. None of us want a life of wood, hay, or stubble. Abiding in Jesus and doing His work His way with His values and character brings praise and reward from Him.

Jesus's rewards are infinitely more valuable than anything this world can offer. Crowns, treasures, and rewards are words the New Testament uses to reveal the reality of Jesus's reward system. Though we do not know the details, just like we don't know the details of the ultimate reality of spending eternity in His presence, we know Who He is. We know His words are true.

## Multiplying Leaders Modeled

How did Jesus take a political radical, a national traitor who raised money for the Romans, small-business owners, doubters, self-centered and personally ambitious followers and make them into a band that turned the world upside down? He changed their perspective from the here and now to the present and forever kingdom. He demonstrated what leading in His kingdom is all about and teaching them the simplicity of leading in His kingdom. He affirmed their faith and admonished their fears. He rebuked their selfishness yet was patient with them as they grew in leading in His kingdom.

He did not transfer content to them at a head level. He did not teach them programs, methods, or procedures. But He did teach them to serve people, meet needs in faith, and die to themselves. Jesus, the Lord, the One who came to show us the way, intentionally built leaders not masses. He personally spent time with individuals and small groups. He built into them the seven realities for kingdom leaders.

When I came into the kingdom, I had to start over. I had to unlearn much of what I learned in business and military leadership. Manipulative practices and command and control leadership are out of bounds for Jesus's leaders. I had to learn (and I am still learning) to move away from fleshly patterns, values, motives, and strategies of the world and move toward His ways of leading and developing people. The practices, values, character, motives, heart, and goals for leading are radically different in Jesus's kingdom.

Fortunately, there were people who helped me learn the ways of Jesus. They taught me to multiply. I learned that the way of Jesus is to develop others, who develop others, who develop others…

**Focused Action Mandated**

God has a heart for the nations. People from every nation, tribe, and tongue will be in His kingdom. From Genesis 11 through Revelation 21 the Three-in-One pursues people, calling out individuals and families to follow Him. Jesus made it clear that this mandate is for leaders in His kingdom.

I recently attended Issachar Summit, a movement of ministries, financial givers, and leaders committed to finishing the task of proclaiming the Gospel to the ends of the earth. In our day it is possible. At the Summit I learned that there are four thousand languages with no Bible; over three thousand unreached people groups; one million villages with no church; and over 3.5 billion Muslims, Buddhists, and Hindus with few workers. At the same time, 99.7 percent of giving is focused on building and maintaining the church where it is while only 0.3 percent of giving is toward extending the reach of the church.

One can deduce from the facts, that we do not have Jesus's focus for action at the front of our hearts, minds, giving, and activities. The global church with its 2.3 billion Christians, five million churches, forty-three thousand denominations, and twelve million workers, could make a real difference in reaching the unreached and planting churches among the unchurched if we take seriously Jesus's mandate.

"As you go into all the world make disciples." Evaluate your ministry and see how aligned you are with Jesus's mandate.

- Where do you focus your ministry activities?
- What people groups are you reaching?
- What percentage of your ministry's activity is focused on reaching the nations?
- What percentage of your ministry's budget goes toward Jesus's mandate for action?

- Where do you focus your personal giving?
- What do you pray for?

Answers to these questions reveal our orientation to His mandate. Remember, when each of us stands before Jesus, He will audit us based on His criteria not ours. Wisdom tells us we should do all we can to align ourselves with His heart and burden.

## No Exemptions

My daughter is a CPA (certified public accountant), as is my brother and brother-in-law. My mother-in-law taught accounting at Virginia Tech for several decades. I am surrounded by accountants. Every year in the United States, we file personal tax returns—we call it a 1040. There is a term in our 1040 called an "exemption." An exemption means that there is no tax on a certain amount (e.g., for children living in one's home). We are taxed on many other items, but we can claim our exemptions as tax free.

We leaders often think we can claim exemptions from the Lord. Because we sacrifice so much, we work so hard, our families sacrifice so much, and we have such importance in the Christian world, we will have an exemption when Jesus audits us. Of course each us of who reads or teaches the Bible would verbally deny this, but practically, we think we are better than the guy with the smaller ministry, the guy who believes differently, or the guy who doesn't do as much mission work as we do. We rank order what is most important in ministry and often put ourselves at the top. What we believe is better, what our church or ministry is doing is better, or what our mission is about is better. These lists mean we are expecting the Lord to give us exemptions for some of what we do or believe.

We may be focused and called to a specific people, nation, or group, but that does not mean we are exempt from aspects of ministry outside our focus. These statements serve as examples:

- I am primarily involved in evangelism and discipleship but not exempt from good deeds.
- I am personally called to serve in a local church but not exempt from extending the Gospel to the ends of the earth (Acts 1:8).
- I am primarily involved in serving the poor but not exempt from making disciples.

Jesus is not impressed that we are charismatic, reformed, Anglican, Baptist, or whatever. Jesus is not impressed that our ministry is larger than another's or that we taught or preached to larger crowds than another. Jesus evaluates according to His criteria not ours—His values, not the world's.

Each of us is evaluated according to Jesus's standards. What we think, what our denomination or church or ministry thinks is not the standard. Even what our "senior pastor" or boss says is not the standard. What some teacher, writer, pastor, or speaker says is not the standard. The standard is what Jesus says, and it is clear in the pages of the New Testament. It is clear in the teachings and ministry of Jesus Himself and His early apostles. Jesus will evaluate us based on His criteria—no exemptions allowed.

**Prayer**
*Lord Jesus, I want to live and lead faithfully in your kingdom. My highest ambition is to hear, "Well done, good and faithful servant." (2 Tim. 4:7–8)*

**Questions for Thought or Discussion**
1. This chapter reviews the book from another angle. What was most helpful from this summary?
2. What is the Spirit saying to you from this book overall?
3. What steps will you take next week to begin applying what is most important now?

# Epilogue

It is a privilege to have served as a guide though this book. My joy is to make this available to as many as possible. Paperback and Kindle versions can be purchased through Amazon.com. Like I mentioned in the introduction, all royalties go to a special account in MentorLink International dedicated to help fund leaders and ministries in the developing world who are focused on multiplying Christlike leaders. For my brothers and sisters who cannot afford to purchase this book or do not have the financial or logistical means to get a copy, it is available as a free PDF download from www.MentorLink.org.

I have shared my heart in these pages. The topics and issues raised are of eternal importance to each of us. My goal has been to help you hear the words of Jesus when you stand before Him, "Well done, good and faithful servant."

Paul said to Timothy, "For the time will come when they will not endure sound doctrine; but wanting their ears tickled, they will accumulate for themselves teachers in accordance to their own desires…" (2 Tim4:3). The pages of this book are not intended to tickle ears. Rather they are of eternal importance to thrust us toward Jesus for how He wants us to lead in His kingdom. He is the One who will audit us according to His standards.

The pages of this book are designed to move you to greater alignment with Jesus and His ways of leading in His kingdom. Only you know how well I have served this purpose in your life.

I recommend using the Leader's Covenant to periodically think and pray through your life as a leader. I also recommend taking a group through this book to discuss it over a number of meetings. It will strengthen you and them as well.

I leave you with Jesus's words:

> If anyone wishes to come after Me, he must deny himself, and take up his cross and follow Me. For whoever wishes to save his life will lose it; but whoever loses his life for My sake will find it. For what will it profit a man if he gains the whole world and forfeits his soul? Or what will a man give in exchange for his soul? For the Son of Man is going to come in the glory of His Father with His angels, and will then repay every man according to his deeds. (Matt 16:24–27)

Until He comes or takes us home, let us faithfully press on serving Him.

Stacy T. Rinehart

> "For we do not preach ourselves but Christ Jesus as Lord and ourselves as your bondservants for Jesus's sake." (2 Cor. 4:5)

# Appendix A

## Transformational Value Shifts

**Leaving behind leadership values and practices of the flesh**

**Pursuing leadership values and practices of the Spirit**

| | |
|---|---|
| **BUILDING MY EMPIRE**<br><br>Believing and acting as if God is primarily at work in the world through me, my ministry, or my organization; believing and acting independently of other Christians as if they are "less important." | **BUILDING GOD'S KINGDOM**<br><br>Having a personal and holistic understanding of the kingdom of God and a perspective that seeks the glory of Christ and the promotion of His Kingdom worldwide. |
| **ENVIRONMENTS OF CONTROL**<br><br>Living and leading in a performance-based or controlling environment which can produce competitiveness, critical attitudes, self-righteous pride and/or burnout. | **ENVIRONMENTS OF GRACE**<br><br>Leadership based on the finished work of Christ; living and leading in humility, openness, and love; treating others with acceptance, forgiveness, honesty, and embracing accountability. |
| **POWER-BASED LEADERSHIP**<br><br>Leading primarily through position, power, and political influence; often relying on manipulation or organizational authority; a lack of trust and of empowering of others. | **SERVANT LEADERSHIP**<br><br>Leading and influencing others through authentic relationships, integrity, and service; giving oneself to meet the needs of others and empowering them to succeed. |
| **ELISTISM AND SELF-SUFFICIENCY**<br><br>Attempting to be personally competent in every area of leadership responsibility; living as a stressed and relationally distant leader; difficulty working together as part of the Body. | **COLLABORATION AND COMMUNITY**<br><br>Leading as part of a team that cooperates together to carry out God's work; influencing through relationships, mutual accountability, delegation, and the empowerment of others. |
| **ACCIDENTALLY ADDING OTHER LEADERS**<br><br>Small and inadequate numbers of leaders are developed through a reliance primarily on formal or formulaic programs. This is rooted in a focus on the *quantitative* (numbers and visible results). | **INTENTIONALLY MULTIPLYING LEADERS**<br><br>Multiplying leadership growth through the mentoring of gifted, reproducing leaders whose hearts' desire and commitment is to humbly and strategically expand God's kingdom (*qualitative*). |

The following is a personal assessment of each value shift developed and refined over many years and nations as part of the *Passing It On!* manual. It's a tool designed to bring each value shift down to every leader's real world. No one is perfectly either operating in the flesh or in the Spirit, but rather operating somewhere between. The scale allows us to see where we are. Take a minute to rate yourself with a number from 1 (operating in the flesh) to 10 (operating in the Spirit).

# Transformational Value #1
# Personal Assessment

Assess where you are in your thinking, values, and practice in the transformational value below. Circle the number in the center column that best pinpoints where you are regarding each pair of statements. For example, give yourself a 1 if the statement in the left column represents you most of the time, a 10 if the right column so fits, or a 5 if you are halfway between. Also respond to the below reflection questions.

| Building My Empire | ... to ... | Building God's Kingdom |
|---|---|---|
| I don't have a clear idea about the kingdom of God and its values | **Understanding God's Kingdom** 1-2-3-4-**5**-6-7-8-9-**10** | I understand the kingdom of God and I want to build it, no matter what it costs me |
| I tend to view my ministry, my business, my church, my family, etc, as the Kingdom of God. God has given these to me | **Ownership** 1-2-3-4-**5**-6-7-8-9-**10** | My ministry, business, church, family, etc belong to God. He gives and He can take away. I will bless His name anyway |
| I want to be noticed. So my ministry is all about my looking good and building my own reputation | **The Glory** 1-2-3-4-**5**-6-7-8-9-**10** | The ministry is all about God. My deepest desire is that He be honored and glorified |
| For success, I should get credit. For failure, others should be blamed | **Success & Failure** 1-2-3-4-**5**-6-7-8-9-**10** | God gets all the credit for success and I take the blame for my mistakes and failures |
| I devote most of my time and energy to building my own kingdom | **Priorities** 1-2-3-4-**5**-6-7-8-9-**10** | I spend most of my time and energy in building Christ's kingdom |
| I don't have the interest, time, or resources for partnering. I see my ministry as competing against other ministers and ministries | **Partnering** 1-2-3-4-**5**-6-7-8-9-**10** | I work in partnership because God blesses when His body functions together cooperatively |
| Prayer is a good idea, but I am too busy to make prayer a priority | **Prayer Priority** 1-2-3-4-**5**-6-7-8-9-**10** | I have so many important things to do that I must give priority to prayer |
| To meet the expectations of people I am called to serve, I engage myself totally in ministry to them | **Expectations** 1-2-3-4-**5**-6-7-8-9-**10** | I educate my people to align their expectations to God's great kingdom expectations |

## Questions for Thought and Discussion

1. In which of the above areas are you doing well? How is God encouraging you from this?
2. Based on your personal assessment regarding this transformational value shift, what is God saying to you about changes you need to make?
3. What keeps you "anchored" in the left-hand column? What fears? What past experiences? What pressures or stresses? What aspects of your culture are barriers to change? What is holding you back?
4. What would real repentance look like on your part? What specific changes in your lifestyle, ministry, or leadership approach would you need to implement?
5. What will the results of my ministry be at the end of my life if I do not make any changes? How satisfying are these results from a kingdom perspective?

# Transformational Value #2
## Personal Assessment

Assess where you are in your thinking, values, and practice in the transformational value below. Circle the number in the center column that best pinpoints where you are regarding each pair of statements. For example, give yourself a 1 if the statement in the left column represents you most of the time, a 10 if the right column so fits, or a 5 if you are halfway between. Also respond to the below reflection questions.

| Environments of Control | ... to... | Environments of Grace |
|---|---|---|
| I feel God is a harsh taskmaster who is distant, absent and hard to please | **View of God**<br>*1-2-3-4-5-6-7-8-9-10* | God is my loving Father, my 'Papa' whose Son suffered death to rescue me and made me His own |
| The key to lasting life change is trying harder to please Him | **Growth**<br>*1-2-3-4-5-6-7-8-9-10* | The key to real transformation is a deepening relationship with the Trinity |
| I always struggle with a sense of guilt as a failure before God | **Forgiveness**<br>*1-2-3-4-5-6-7-8-9-10* | I always feel forgiven & deeply loved by my God & Savior |
| Holy living isn't that important. Real people make mistakes | **Holy Living**<br>*1-2-3-4-5-6-7-8-9-10* | Holiness is important, but it is only possible as we walk in intimacy with God |
| I am driven by shame and/or guilt | **Shame & Identity**<br>*1-2-3-4-5-6-7-8-9-10* | I know I am a beloved child of God |
| As Christians, we need rules to keep going straight | **Rules/Law**<br>*1-2-3-4-5-6-7-8-9-10* | We need God's rules (not men's) to continually bring us to the cross |
| I have no practical understanding of who the Holy Spirit is and how to walk in Him | **Holy Spirit**<br>*1-2-3-4-5-6-7-8-9-10* | I am learning to enjoy precious intimacy with God through the indwelling Holy Spirit |
| To be honest, at times I'm very proud of my gifts, abilities and accomplishments | **My "Boast" #1**<br>*1-2-3-4-5-6-7-8-9-10* | I am proud of the great price Jesus paid to make people like me part of His family |
| In comparison to others, I am often ashamed of my gifts, abilities and accomplishments | **My "Boast" #2**<br>*1-2-3-4-5-6-7-8-9-10* | As His beloved child, I am learning to boast only in what Christ does in and through me by faith |
| Successful ministry can only take place by ministering and leading out of my strengths | **Brokenness**<br>*1-2-3-4-5-6-7-8-9-10* | Significant ministry usually takes place by ministering and leading out of weakness, brokenness and transparency |
| Prayer is a burdensome duty that I feel I must do in order to please God | **Attitude in Prayer**<br>*1-2-3-4-5-6-7-8-9-10* | Prayer is a privilege, in which the Holy Spirit joins me with my Father and His Son in loving communion |

**Questions for Thought and Discussion**

1. In which of the above areas are you doing well? How is God encouraging you from this?

2. Based on your personal assessment regarding this transformational value shift, what is God saying to you about changes you need to make?

3. What keeps you "anchored" in the left-hand column? What fears? What past experiences? What pressures or stresses? What aspects of your culture are barriers to change? What is holding you back?

4. What would real repentance look like on your part? What specific changes in your lifestyle, ministry, or leadership approach would you need to implement?

5. What will the results of my ministry be at the end of my life if I do not make any changes? How satisfying are these results from a kingdom perspective?

# Transformational Value #3
# Personal Assessment

Assess where you are in your thinking, values, and practice in the transformational value below. Circle the number in the center column that best pinpoints where you are regarding each pair of statements. For example, give yourself a 1 if the statement in the left column represents you most of the time, a 10 if the right column so fits, or a 5 if you are halfway between. Also respond to the below reflection questions.

| Power-Based Leadership | ... to... | Servant Leadership |
|---|---|---|
| In doing ministry with others, I give more importance to the task than to relationships | **Relationship versus Task** 1-2-3-4-5-6-7-8-9-10 | In ministry, both relationship and task are essential components. Our unity as God's people is key to our impact |
| I draw my leadership authority primarily from my job description, title and our organization's flow chart | **Authority** 1-2-3-4-5-6-7-8-9-10 | My authority rests primarily on a spiritual authority based on trust, relationship, integrity and ministry |
| Respect comes primarily with my title and the position I hold | **Respect** 1-2-3-4-5-6-7-8-9-10 | Respect is primarily earned as I serve Christ, His purposes and His people |
| I expect to get the credit I deserve for the work I have led our group in doing well – that is success | **Leadership Success** 1-2-3-4-5-6-7-8-9-10 | Success is equipping and empowering my teammates such that we accomplish His work to His glory |
| As a leader, I use direct control of every aspect of our operation, using people as needed to ensure success | **Control 1** 1-2-3-4-5-6-7-8-9-10 | God is in control. I cooperate with Him in developing and helping faithful people who are trusted to do their part |
| I like to be involved in all communications between my staff members as well as in important decision-making | **Control 2** 1-2-3-4-5-6-7-8-9-10 | I decentralize decision making, such that trusted teammates have the freedom to act in line with the plans we have determined as a team |
| In our work group, I make sure that everyone including outsiders know that I am the leader in charge | **Leadership Profile** 1-2-3-4-5-6-7-8-9-10 | An outside observer may not easily know I am the team leader. We practice a shared leadership based on one's giftedness in any given area |
| As a leader my role is to influence the people I lead by keeping as many of them happy as possible | **People Pleasing** 1-2-3-4-5-6-7-8-9-10 | In serving Christ, His kingdom cause, and His people, I must sometimes make hard decisions that make some friends unhappy |
| I spend very little time actually praying with and/or for the people under my leadership | **Prayer Leadership** 1-2-3-4-5-6-7-8-9-10 | I pray regularly with and for those I lead since it encourages and empowers them in the Lord |

**Questions for Thought and Discussion**

1. In which of the above areas are you doing well? How is God encouraging you from this?

2. Based on your personal assessment regarding this transformational value shift, what is God saying to you about changes you need to make?

3. What keeps you "anchored" in the left-hand column? What fears? What past experiences? What pressures or stresses? What aspects of your culture are barriers to change? What is holding you back?

4. What would real repentance look like on your part? What specific changes in your lifestyle, ministry, or leadership approach would you need to implement?

5. What will the results of my ministry be at the end of my life if I do not make any changes? How satisfying are these results from a kingdom perspective?

# Transformational Value #4
# Personal Assessment

Assess where you are in your thinking, values, and practice in the transformational value below. Circle the number in the center column that best pinpoints where you are regarding each pair of statements. For example, give yourself a 1 if the statement in the left column represents you most of the time, a 10 if the right column so fits, or a 5 if you are halfway between. Also respond to the below reflection questions.

| Elitism and Self-Sufficiency | … to… | Collaboration and Community |
|---|---|---|
| I find teamwork costs too much. There are inborn "efficiencies" in each of us working on our own | **Working Together** 1-2-3-4-**5**-6-7-8-9-**10** | Working together both delights God and blesses the team. To me, teamwork is worth its cost |
| A good leader must be a loner. I am accountable to God alone and trust in Him alone for protection | **Loneliness** 1-2-3-4-**5**-6-7-8-9-**10** | As a leader, I value a team, not only for ministry effectiveness but also for my own safety and growth |
| I don't show weakness nor am I open for criticism or correction, because then people will not follow me | **Weakness** 1-2-3-4-**5**-6-7-8-9-**10** | I try to lead through brokenness and transparency as it builds community and releases God's power |
| As a leader, I try to have all of the answers and possess all the needed gifts to carry out our mission | **All-competent** 1-2-3-4-**5**-6-7-8-9-**10** | As a leader, I need a team that helps to find answers and complements the gift-mix required to succeed |
| As a leader, I deserve credit for my success. This naturally builds a good reputation and track record | **Credit** 1-2-3-4-**5**-6-7-8-9-**10** | As a leader I give glory to God, by crediting my team members for any success that God allows |
| As a leader I know that success today opens doors for greater ministry opportunity tomorrow | **One's Career** 1-2-3-4-**5**-6-7-8-9-**10** | I leave my career in God's hands, recognizing that He gives us our work and requires only faithfulness |
| In our team, everyone seems to be wearing a protective mask. We don't feel safe enough to open up | **Safe Place** 1-2-3-4-**5**-6-7-8-9-**10** | Our team is becoming a relational safe place where there is freedom to show and share our weaknesses |
| I like everyone to work on their own. After all, we each have other places where we get Christian fellowship | **Healing Family** 1-2-3-4-**5**-6-7-8-9-**10** | Our team is becoming like a family. We really help one another in our individual growth in the Lord |
| We rarely pray together. When we pray, it seems mechanical and ineffective. I just don't know how to make it better | **Prayer as a Team** 1-2-3-4-**5**-6-7-8-9-**10** | Prayer changes things so we have made it a team priority. We pray regularly for and with one another |

**Questions for Thought and Discussion**

1. In which of the above areas are you doing well? How is God encouraging you from this?

2. Based on your personal assessment regarding this transformational value shift, what is God saying to you about changes you need to make?

3. What keeps you "anchored" in the left-hand column? What fears? What past experiences? What pressures or stresses? What aspects of your culture are barriers to change? What is holding you back?

4. What would real repentance look like on your part? What specific changes in your lifestyle, ministry, or leadership approach would you need to implement?

5. What will the results of my ministry be at the end of my life if I do not make any changes? How satisfying are these results from a kingdom perspective?

# Transformational Value #5
# Personal Assessment

Assess where you are in your thinking, values, and practice in the transformational value below. Circle the number in the center column that best pinpoints where you are regarding each pair of statements. For example, give yourself a 1 if the statement in the left column represents you most of the time, a 10 if the right column so fits, or a 5 if you are halfway between. Also respond to the below reflection questions.

| Accidental Addition | ... to... | Intentional Multiplication |
|---|---|---|
| Winning and growing of significant numbers of people is my dream. I want to be in control | **Vision for Multiplication** 1-2-3-4-5-6-7-8-9-10 | My vision is to see many come to Christ by equipping reproducing leaders who are able to expand and lead movements |
| The quantitative growth to one's ministry is the most important aspect of ministry success | **Allure of Numbers** 1-2-3-4-5-6-7-8-9-10 | The qualitative growth of a small number of reproducing leaders is key to long term multiplication |
| I don't have the skill, interest and time to mentor emerging leaders. I am just too busy | **Priority of Mentoring** 1-2-3-4-5-6-7-8-9-10 | I make mentoring of emerging leaders a priority since it is the key to long-term effectiveness |
| I enjoy using my gifts so much that I just can't give the ministry away to emerging leaders | **Ministry Fulfillment** 1-2-3-4-5-6-7-8-9-10 | I sacrifice some of my own personal fulfillment for the joy of seeing young leaders blossom |
| We will mostly utilize people trained at Bible schools or by others to lead our ministry | **Leadership Development** 1-2-3-4-5-6-7-8-9-10 | We train our own leaders with a focus on the whole person: hearts, skills, and knowledge |
| We can impart biblical knowledge and ministry skills through a leadership training program | **Character Transformation** 1-2-3-4-5-6-7-8-9-10 | We mentor people, as it is the key to molding godly character. This is central to leading effectively |
| We need more leaders, but I am so busy with my ministry that there is not enough time to do it | **Intentionality** 1-2-3-4-5-6-7-8-9-10 | I am very intentional about pouring my life into potential leaders, a key to ministry growth |
| I believe in prayer but I don't seem to have the time, energy and skill to make it central to what I'm doing | **Prayer for Multiplication** 1-2-3-4-5-6-7-8-9-10 | Great movements of God have always been an answer to prayer, so prayer mobilization is a core part of our strategy |

**Questions for Thought and Discussion**

1. In which of the above areas are you doing well? How is God encouraging you from this?

2. Based on your personal assessment regarding this transformational value shift, what is God saying to you about changes you need to make?

3. What keeps you "anchored" in the left-hand column? What fears? What past experiences? What pressures or stresses? What aspects of your culture are barriers to change? What is holding you back?

4. What would real repentance look like on your part? What specific changes in your lifestyle, ministry, or leadership approach would you need to implement?

5. What will the results of my ministry be at the end of my life if I do not make any changes? How satisfying are these results from a kingdom perspective?

# Appendix B

## New Testament Leaders

| Label | Primary Passages | Clear Examples | Functions & Characteristics |
|---|---|---|---|
| Apostle | 1 Cor. 12:28<br>Eph. 4:11<br>Many others: we know more about the gift of apostle than all the other gifts combined. | The Eleven<br>Apollos<br>Barnabas<br>James<br>Paul<br>Timothy<br>Titus | 1. Innovating and pioneering new ministries.<br>2. Correcting existing ministries.<br>3. Completing what is lacking in existing ministries.<br>4. Usually mobile in their ministries.<br>5. Trans-local ministry oversight and influence. |
| Prophet | Rom. 12:6<br>1 Cor. 12:28<br>Eph. 4:11 | Agabus<br>Phillip's daughters<br>Barnabas<br>Judas<br>Silas | 1. Sees issues and implications clearly and speaks to them forcefully.<br>2. Corrective of existing ministries.<br>3. Often predicts upcoming events. |
| Evangelist | Eph. 4:11 | Phillip<br>Paul | 1. Constantly reaching out to the lost.<br>2. See issues related to reaching the lost. |
| Shepherd | Eph. 4:11 | | 1. Constantly ministering to & guiding the saved.<br>2. Sees issues primarily related to building up the saved. |
| Teacher | Rom. 12:7<br>1 Cor. 12:28<br>Eph. 4:11 | Paul | 1. Constantly studying the Scriptures.<br>2. Focused primarily on understanding and propagating right living based on the Bible. |
| Leader / Ruler | Rom. 12:8 | Peter<br>James<br>Paul | 1. Tends to see a direction to take in the midst of complex issues.<br>2. Constantly serving a group of believers. |

Note: The New Testament does not leave us without describing and illustrating what leaders in Jesus's kingdom are to be and do.

Taken from *Upside Down: The Paradox of Servant Leadership,* Navpress, 1998, p. 107.

# Appendix C

## THE RELATIONAL NATURE OF SPIRITUAL LEADERSHIP

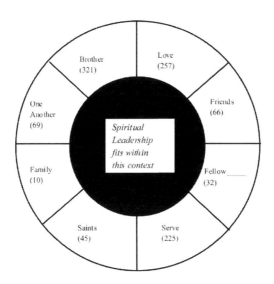

Note: The number listed under the term is the number of times the term occurs in the New Testament.

The point here is that whatever else spiritual leadership is, it must fit within this context to be authentic leadership in Jesus's kingdom.

Taken from *Upside Down: The Paradox of Servant Leadership*, Navpress, 1998, p. 105.

# Appendix D

**Matthew**
5:19
7:15–23
9:1–13
12:9–14, 22–45
13:24–30, 36–43
15:1–20
16:1–12, 23
21:12–16, 23–46
22:1–46
23:1–36
24:4–5, 23–25
26:3–5, 20–25, 47–50, 57–68
27:20
28:11–15

**Mark**
2:15–17, 23–28

3:1–6, 22–30
7:1–16
8:11–16, 31–53
10:2
11:15–18, 27–33
12:1–40
13:21–22
14:17–21, 43–46, 55–65
15:1–15

**Luke**
5:17–26, 29–39
6:1–11
7:30, 36–50
10:25–37
11:15–26, 37–54
12:1–3
13:10–17, 31–33

14:1–6
15:1–2
16:14–16
19:36–40, 45–48
20:1–8, 19–47
22:1–6, 47–53, 66–23:5
23:10

**John**
2:12–22
5:10–18
7:25–36, 40–53
8:1–11, 13, 48–59
9:13–34, 40–41
10:22–39
11:47–57
12:4–11, 19, 42–43
13:21–24

18:1–14, 19–24
19:1–16

**Acts**
4:1–22
5:17–42
6:8–8:3
8:9–24
9:23–25
13:45
15:1–5
20:28–31

**Romans**
16:17–18

**1 Corinthians**
3:1–15

**2 Corinthians**
10:1–18
11:4–15, 20

**Galatians**
1:6–10
2:4–5, 11–21
5:1–12
6:12–13

**Ephesians**
4:14
Philippians
1:15–17
3:17–19

**Colossians**
2:8, 18–19

**1 Thessalonians**
2:5–6

**2 Thessalonians**
2:1–3

**1 Timothy**
1:6–7, 19–20
4:1–3
6:3–5

**2 Timothy**
1:15–18
3:6–9, 13
4:3–4, 10, 14–15

**Titus**
1:10–14, 16

**Hebrews**
13:9

**1 Peter**
5:2–3

**2 Peter**
2:1–22
3:17

**1 John**
2:18–19
4:1–6

**2 John**
7–11

**3 John**
9–11

**Jude**
3–23

**Revelation**
2:1–7, 12–17, 18–29

## Suggestions

1. Scan each reference looking for doctrinal, character, and ministry false leaders.
2. Investigate the strategies false leaders use to gain or maintain influence and control.

# Suggested Resources

**MentorLink Institute**—a systematic way for existing and emerging leaders to grow in the foundations and practices of mentoring and multiplying Christlike disciples and leaders for the kingdom. Each module has a participants' and facilitators' guide. See www.MentorLink.org for more information or to become a participant.

I suggest that you sign up for the mentor orientation through the institute. With this experience, you will have the tools needed to start mentoring and multiplying leaders.

*Passing It On* is a seminar-format expansion of chapter 2. In addition, it leads participants toward a lifestyle of mentoring and multiplying Christlike disciples and leaders. The manual can be acquired at www. MentorLink.org and used in any group.

*Upside Down: The Paradox of Servant Leadership* (NavPress, 1998), by Stacy Rinehart. This book builds the foundation of Spiritual leadership for God's people from the words of Jesus and His apostles.

**The Leader's Covenant** is available in multiple languages at www. MentorLink.org.

41728500R00105

Made in the USA
Middletown, DE
21 March 2017